The Brief Student Guide to DSM-5

JOEL O. GOLDBERG

WILEY

Production Credits
Vice President & Publisher: Veronica Visentin
Acquisitions Editor: Rodney Burke
Marketing Manager: Patty Maher
Editorial Manager: Karen Staudinger
Production Manager: Tegan Wallace
Developmental Editor: Andrea Grzybowski
Editorial Assistant: Luisa Begani
Cover Design: Tegan Wallace

Library and Archives Canada Cataloguing in Publication
Cataloguing data available from Library and Archives Canada

Printing & Binding: Friesens
Printed and bound in Canada
1 2 3 4 5 FP 18 17 16 15 14

John Wiley & Sons Canada, Ltd
5353 Dundas St. W., Suite 400
Toronto, ON M9A 6H8

Visit our website at www.wiley.ca

TABLE OF CONTENTS

INTRODUCTION

The purpose of this booklet is to familiarize the student of abnormal psychology with the *Diagnostic and Statistical Manual of Mental Disorders: Fifth Edition* (or *DSM-5*; American Psychiatric Association, 2013) which is considered to be the authoritative guide to diagnosing psychopathology.

Why do we do we need to have a classification system for mental disorders? It is important for a number of reasons that are shared by all scientific fields (e.g., biology) which describe their objects of study. Classification is essential for communication (so we can agree that we are talking about the same thing), to organize information into standardized definitions, to describe the characteristics of phenomena, to make predictions (such as indications for specific kinds of treatment), and to provide a basis for understanding the person and furthering the scientific field through research.

When there is little consensus over the core symptoms and features of mental disorders, then scientists and practitioners with different theoretical orientations cannot share ideas, discoveries and insights. The hope for developing a good classification system is that it will improve understanding, not add to stigma, and that it will move us further along the road to effective treatment and eventual cures.

Like previous editions of the DSM, the latest DSM manual provides specific criteria sets for each disorder; however, each edition since 1844 has attempted to provide revisions based on identified limitations and shortcomings and in response to advances in knowledge. Important criticisms include the manual's focus on the presence or absence of symptoms rather than on the origins of those symptoms and associated treatment implications; its adherence to a "medical model" of mental health care rather than to more client-centred perspectives; and its adoption of a categorical instead of a more dimensional approach to diagnosis. The debate about including dimensional understandings, including those which cut across diagnostic category boundaries, contributed to the introduction of a new section of the latest manual which outlines what are called emerging measures and models, many of which more clearly incorporate dimensional approaches to diagnosis as well as the addition for diagnosticians to specify current severity (e.g., mild, moderate, severe).

For those who were familiar with the previous version, the *DSM-5* introduces some key changes, including the elimination of what was termed the multi-axial system. An attempt has been made to address concerns about the previously limited focus on cross-cultural factors and diversity through the inclusion in the *DSM-5* of culture-related diagnostic issues for each category and a cultural formulation outline in Section III. Critics of this latest version, however, are concerned that so-called normal problems of everyday life have become diagnosable conditions. Indeed, the sheer number of diagnostic categories identified in successive editions continues to increase, due in part to advances in our knowledge, but also due to the labeling of phenomenon (such as the proposed caffeine use disorder) which may or may not be considered psychopathology.

The DSM provides a snapshot in time, representing the current state of the field of psychopathology for routine clinical use in following the agreed-upon diagnostic criteria for mental disorders. This picture will continue to change with improvements in our methods of assessment and evaluation, with developments in our theoretical understandings and advances in our knowledge based upon scientific research.

OVERVIEW OF DSM-5 CLASSIFICATION CATEGORIES

Here is an overview of the main classification categories in Section II of the DSM-5 classification system with the main diagnoses for each category. This provides a kind of aerial view of the landscape of the kinds of mental health conditions that people could experience in their lifetimes from childhood to late adulthood.

NEURODEVELOPMENTAL DISORDERS

Intellectual Disability
Communication Disorders
Autism Spectrum Disorder
Attention-Deficit/Hyperactivity Disorder
Specific Learning Disorder
Motor Disorders

SCHIZOPHRENIA SPECTRUM AND OTHER PSYCHOTIC DISORDERS

Schizotypal (Personality) Disorder
Delusional Disorder
Brief Psychotic Disorder
Schizophreniform Disorder
Schizophrenia
Schizoaffective Disorder
Substance/Medication-Induced Psychotic Disorder
Catatonia Associated With Another Mental Disorder

BIPOLAR AND RELATED DISORDERS

Bipolar I Disorder
Bipolar II Disorder
Cyclothymic Disorder

DEPRESSIVE DISORDERS

Disruptive Mood Dysregulation Disorder
Persistent Depressive Disorder (Dysthymia)
Premenstrual Dysphoric Disorder

ANXIETY DISORDERS

Separation Anxiety Disorder
Selective Mutism
Specific Phobia
Social Anxiety Disorder (Social Phobia)
Panic Disorder
Agoraphobia
Generalized Anxiety Disorder

OBSESSIVE-COMPULSIVE AND RELATED DISORDERS

Obsessive-Compulsive Disorder
Body Dysmorphic Disorder
Hoarding Disorder
Trichotillomania (Hair-Pulling Disorder)
Excoriation (Skin-Picking) Disorder

TRAUMA- AND STRESSOR-RELATED DISORDERS

Reactive Attachment Disorder
Disinhibited Social Engagement Disorder
Posttraumatic Stress Disorder
Acute Stress Disorder
Adjustment Disorders

DISSOCIATIVE DISORDER

Dissociative Identity Disorder
Dissociative Amnesia
Depersonalization/Derealization Disorder

SOMATIC SYMPTOM AND RELATED DISORDERS

Somatic Symptom Disorder
Illness Anxiety Disorder
Conversion Disorder (Functional Neurological Symptom Disorder)

PSYCHOLOGICAL FACTORS AFFECTING OTHER MEDICAL CONDITIONS

Factitious Disorder (includes Factitious Disorder Imposed on Self, Factitious Disorder Imposed on Another)

FEEDING AND EATING DISORDERS

Pica
Rumination Disorder
Avoidant/Restrictive Food Intake Disorder
Anorexia Nervosa
Bulimia Nervosa
Binge-Eating Disorder

ELIMINATION DISORDERS

Enuresis
Encopresis

SLEEP-WAKE DISORDERS

Insomnia Disorder
Hypersomnolence Disorder
Narcolepsy
Breathing-Related Sleep Disorders
- Obstructive Sleep Apnea Hypopnea
- Central Sleep Apnea
- Sleep-Related Hypoventilation
- Circadian Rhythm Sleep-Wake Disorders

Parasomnias
- Non-Rapid Eye Movement Sleep Arousal Disorders
- Nightmare Disorder
- Rapid Eye Movement Sleep Behavior Disorder
- Restless Legs Syndrome
- Substance/Medication-Induced Sleep Disorder

SEXUAL DYSFUNCTIONS

Delayed Ejaculation
Erectile Disorder
Female Orgasmic Disorder
Female Sexual Interest/Arousal Disorder
Genito-Pelvic Pain/Penetration Disorder
Male Hypoactive Sexual Desire Disorder
Premature (Early) Ejaculation

GENDER DYSPHORIA

Gender Dysphoria

DISRUPTIVE, IMPULSE-CONTROL, AND CONDUCT DISORDERS

Oppositional Defiant Disorder
Intermittent Explosive Disorder
Conduct Disorder
Antisocial Personality Disorder

SUBSTANCE-RELATED AND ADDICTIVE DISORDERS

ubstance-Related Disorders

lcohol-Related disorders

- Alcohol Use Disorder
- Alcohol Intoxication
- Alcohol Withdrawal

affeine-Related Disorders

- Caffeine Intoxication
- Caffeine Withdrawal

annabis-Related Disorders

- Cannabis Use Disorder
- Cannabis Intoxication
- Cannabis Withdrawal

allucinogen-Related Disorders

- Phencyclidine Use Disorder

nhalant-Related Disorders

pioid-Related Disorders

edative-, Hypnotic-, or Anxiolytic-Related Disorders

NEUROCOGNITIVE DISORDERS

elirium

ajor and Mild Neurocognitive Disorders

- Major or Mild Neurocognitive Disorder Due to Alzheimer's Disease
- Major or Mild Frontotemporal Neurocognitive Disorder
- Major or Mild Neurocognitive Disorder With Lewy Bodies
- Major or Mild Vascular Neurocognitive Disorder
- Major or Mild Neurocognitive Disorder Due to Traumatic Brain Injury
- Substance/Medication-Induce Major or Mild Neurocognitive Disorder
- Major or Mild Neurocognitive Disorder Due to HIV Infection
- Major or Mild Neurocognitive Disorder Due to Parkinson's Disease
- Major or Mild Neurocognitive Disorder Due to Huntington's Disease

PERSONALITY DISORDERS

luster A Personality Disorders

- Paranoid
- Schizoid
- Schizotypal

Cluster B Personality Disorders

- Antisocial
- Borderline
- Histrionic
- Narcissistic

Cluster C Personality Disorders

- Avoidant
- Dependent
- Obsessive Compulsive

PARAPHILIC DISORDERS

Voyeuristic Disorder
Exhibitionistic Disorder
Frotteuristic Disorder
Sexual Masochism Disorder
Sexual Sadism Disorder
Pedophilic Disorder
Fetishistic Disorder
Transvestic Disorder

MEDICATION-INDUCED MOVEMENT DISORDERS AND OTHER ADVERSE EFFECTS OF MEDICATION

Neuroleptic-Induced Parkinsonism
Neuroleptic Malignant Syndrome
Medication-Induced Acute Dystonia
Medication-Induced Acute Akathisia
Tardive Dyskinesia
Tardive Dystonia
Tardive Akathisia
Medication-Induced Postural Tremor
Antidepressant Discontinuation Syndrome

OTHER CONDITIONS THAT MAY BE A FOCUS OF CLINICAL ATTENTION

Relational Problems

Problems Related to Family Upbringing
Other Problems Related to Primary Support Group

Abuse and Neglect

Childhood Physical Abuse
Childhood Sexual Abuse
Child Neglect
Childhood Psychological Abuse

Educational and Occupational Problems

Educational Problems
Academic or Educational Problem
Occupational Problems
Problem Related to Current Military Deployment Status

Housing and Economic Problems

Housing Problems
Homelessness
Inadequate Housing
Discord With Neighbor, Lodger, or Landlord
Problem Related to Living in a Residential Institution
Economic Problems
Lack of Adequate Food or Safe Drinking Water
Extreme Poverty
Low Income
Insufficient Social Insurance or Welfare Support
Unspecified Housing or Economic Problem

Other Problems Related to the Social Environment

Phase of Life Problem
Problem Related to Living Alone
Acculturation Difficulty
Social Exclusion or Rejection
Target of (Perceived) Adverse Discrimination or Persecution

Problems Related to Crime or Interaction With the Legal System

Victim of Crime
Conviction in Civil or Criminal Proceedings Without Imprisonment
Imprisonment or Other Incarceration
Problems Related to Release From Prison
Problems Related to Other Legal Circumstances

Other Health Service Encounters for Counseling and Medical Advice

Sex Counseling
Other Counseling or Consultation

Problems Related to Other Psychosocial, Personal, and Environmental Circumstances

Religious or Spiritual Problem
Problems Related to Unwanted Pregnancy
Problems Related to Multiparity
Discord With Social Service Provider, Including Probation Officer, Case Manager, or Social Services Worker
Victim of Terrorism or Torture
Exposure to Disaster, War, or Other Hostilities

Other Circumstances of Personal History

Other Personal History of Psychological Trauma
Personal History of Self-Harm
Personal History of Military Deployment
Other Personal Risk Factors
Problem Related to Lifestyle
Adult Antisocial Behavior
Child or Adolescent Antisocial Behavior

Problems Related to Access to Medical and Other Health Care

Unavailability or Inaccessibility of Health Care Facilities
Unavailability or Inaccessibility of Other Helping Agencies

Nonadherence to Medical Treatment

Nonadherence to Medical Treatment
Overweight or Obesity
Malingering
Wandering Associated With a Mental Disorder
Borderline Intellectual Functioning

DIAGNOSTIC CRITERIA FOR SELECTED PROPOSED DSM-5 DISORDERS FOR FURTHER STUDY

Here are a few examples of proposed new disorders that are included in the *DSM-V* as conditions being considered for future study. Researchers and practitioners will be evaluating whether there is scientific and clinical value in employing these diagnostic classifications or whether, as critics have noted, using these new categories will lead to over-diagnosing as psychopathology that which is normal in our lives.

Proposed Criteria for Attenuated Psychosis Syndrome

A. At least one of the following symptoms is present in attenuated form, with relatively intact reality testing, and is of sufficient severity or frequency to warrant clinical attention:
   1. Delusions.
   2. Hallucinations.
   3. Disorganized speech.

B. Symptom(s) must have been present at least once per week for the past month.

C. Symptom(s) must have begun or worsened in the past year.

D. Symptom(s) is sufficiently distressing and disabling to the individual to warrant clinical attention.

E. Symptom(s) is not better explained by another mental disorder, including a depressive or bipolar disorder with psychotic features, and is not attributable to the physiological effects of a substance or another medical condition.

F. Criteria for any psychotic disorder have never been met.

Proposed Criteria for Complex Bereavement Disorder

A. The individual experienced the death of someone with whom he or she had a close relationship.

B. Since the death, at least one of the following symptoms is experienced on more days than not and to a clinically significant degree and has persisted for at least 12 months after the death in the case of bereaved adults and 6 months for bereaved children:

1. Persistent yearning/longing for the deceased. In young children, yearning may be expressed in play and behavior, including behaviors that reflect being separated from, and also reuniting with, a caregiver or other attachment figure.
2. Intense sorrow and emotional pain in response to the death.
3. Preoccupation with the deceased.
4. Preoccupation with the circumstances of the death. In children, this preoccupation with the deceased may be expressed through the themes of play and behavior and may extend to preoccupation with possible death or others close to them.

C. Since the death, at least six of the following symptoms are experienced on more days than not and to a clinically significant degree, and have persisted for at least 12 months after the death in the case of bereaved adults and 6 months for bereaved children:

Reactive distress to the death

1. Marked difficulty accepting the death. In children, this is dependent on the child's capacity to comprehend the meaning and permanence of death.
2. Experiencing disbelief or emotional numbness over the loss.
3. Difficulty with positive reminiscing about the deceased.
4. Bitterness or anger related to the loss.
5. Maladaptive appraisals about oneself in relation to the deceased or the death (e.g., self-blame).
6. Excessive avoidance or reminders of the loss (e.g., avoidance of individuals, places, or situations associated with the deceased; in children, this may include avoidance of thoughts and feelings regarding the deceased).

Social/Identity disruption

7. A desire to die in order to be with the deceased.
8. Difficulty trusting other individuals since the death.
9. Feeling alone or detached from other individuals since the death.
10. Feeling that life is meaningless or empty without the deceased, or the belief that one cannot function without the deceased.

11. Confusion about one's role in life, or a diminished sense of one's identity (e.g., feeling that a part of oneself died with the deceased).
12. Difficulty or reluctance to pursue interests since the loss or to plan for the future (e.g., friendships, activities).

D. The disturbance causes clinically significant distress or impairment in social, occupational, or other important areas of functioning.

E. The bereavement reaction is out of proportion to or inconsistent with cultural, religious, or age-appropriate norms.

Specify if:

With traumatic bereavement: Bereavement due to homicide or suicide with persistent distressing preoccupations regarding the traumatic nature of the death (often in response to loss reminders), including the deceased's last moments, degree of suffering and mutilating injury, or the malicious or intentional nature of the death.

Proposed Criteria for Caffeine Use Disorder

A problematic pattern of caffeine use leading to clinically significant impairment or distress, as manifested by at least the first three of the following criteria occurring within a 12-month period:

1. A persistent desire or unsuccessful efforts to cut down or control caffeine use.
2. Continued caffeine use despite knowledge of having a persistent or recurrent physical or psychological problem that is likely to have been caused or exacerbated by caffeine.
3. Withdrawal, as manifested by either of the following:
    a. The characteristic withdrawal syndrome for caffeine.
    b. Caffeine (or a closely related) substance is taken to relieve or avoid withdrawal symptoms.
4. Caffeine is often taken in larger amounts or over a longer period than was intended.
5. Recurrent caffeine use resulting in a failure to fulfill major role obligations at work, school, or home (e.g., repeated tardiness or absences from work or school related to caffeine use or withdrawal).
6. Continued caffeine use despite having persistent or recurrent social or interpersonal problems caused or exacerbated by the effects of caffeine (e.g., arguments with spouse about consequences of use, medical problems, cost).
7. Tolerance, as defined by either of the following:

a. A need for markedly increased amounts of caffeine to achieve desired effect.
b. Markedly diminished effect with continued use of the same amount of caffeine.

8. A great deal of time is spent in activities necessary to obtain caffeine, use caffeine, or recover from its effects.
9. Craving or a strong desire or urge to use caffeine.

Proposed Criteria for Internet Gaming Disorder

Persistent and recurrent use of the Internet to engage in games, often with other players, leading to clinically significant impairment or distress as indicated by five (or more) of the following in a 12-month period:

1. Preoccupation with Internet games. (The individual thinks about previous gaming activity or anticipates playing the next game; Internet gaming becomes the dominant activity in daily life).

Note: This disorder is distinct from Internet gambling, which is included under gambling disorder.

2. Withdrawal symptoms when Internet gaming is taken away. (These symptoms are typically described as irritability, anxiety, or sadness, but there are no physical signs of pharmacological withdrawal.)
3. Tolerance—the need to spend increasing amounts of time engaged in Internet games.
4. Unsuccessful attempts to control the participation in Internet games.
5. Loss of interests in previous hobbies and entertainment as a result of, and with the exception of, Internet games.
6. Continued excessive use of Internet games despite knowledge of psychosocial problems.
7. Has deceived family members, therapists, or others regarding the amount of Internet gaming.
8. Use of Internet games to escape or relieve a negative mood (e.g., feelings of helplessness, guilt, anxiety).
9. Has jeopardized or lost a significant relationship, job, or educational or career opportunity because of participation in Internet games.

Note: Only nongambling Internet games are included in this disorder. Use of the Internet for required activities in a business or profession is not included; nor is the disorder intended to include other recreational or social Internet use. Similarly, sexual internet sites are excluded.

Specify current severity:

Internet gaming disorder can be mild, moderate, or severe depending on the degree or disruption of normal activities. Individuals with less severe internet gaming disorder may exhibit fewer symptoms and less disruption of their lives. Those with severe internet gaming disorder will have more hours spent on the computer and more severe loss of relationships or career or school opportunities.

Proposed New Diagnostic Criteria for Antisocial Personality Disorder

A. Moderate or greater impairment in personality functioning, manifested by characteristic difficulties in two or more of the following four areas:

1. ***Identity:*** Egocentrism; self-esteem derived from personal gain, power, or pleasure.
2. ***Self-direction:*** Goal setting based on personal gratification; absence of prosocial internal standards, associated with failure to conform to lawful or culturally normative ethical behavior.
3. ***Empathy:*** Lack of concern for feelings, needs, or suffering of others; lack of remorse after hurting or mistreating another.
4. ***Intimacy:*** Incapacity for mutually intimate relationships, as exploitation is a primary means of relating to others, including by deceit and coercion; use of dominance or intimidation to control others.

B. Six or more of the following seven pathological personality traits:

1. ***Manipulativeness*** (an aspect of **Antagonism**): Frequent use of subterfuge to influence or control others; use of seduction, charm, glibness, or ingratiation to achieve one's ends.
2. ***Callousness*** (an aspect of **Antagonism**): Lack of concern for feelings or problems of others; lack of guilt or remorse about the negative or harmful effects of one's actions on others; aggression; sadism.
3. ***Deceitfulness*** (an aspect of **Antagonism**): Dishonesty and fraudulence; misrepresentation of self; embellishment or fabrication when relating events.
4. ***Hostility*** (an aspect of **Antagonism**): Persistent or frequent angry feelings; anger or irritability in response to minor slights and insults; mean, nasty, or vengeful behavior.
5. ***Risk taking*** (an aspect of **Antagonism**): Engagement in dangerous, risky, and potentially self-damaging activities, unnecessarily and without regard for consequences; boredom

proneness and thoughtless initiation of activities to counter boredom; lack of concern for one's limitations and denial of the reality of personal danger.

6. ***Impulsivity*** (an aspect of **Antagonism**): Acting on the spur of the moment in response to immediate stimuli; acting on momentary basis without a plan or consideration of outcomes; difficulty establishing and following plans.
7. ***Irresponsibility*** (an aspect of **Antagonism**): Disregard for—and failure to honor—financial and other obligations or commitments; lack of respect for—and lack of follow-through on—agreements and promises.

Note. The individual is at least 18 years of age.

Specify if:

With psychopathic features

Proposed New Diagnostic Criteria for Borderline Personality Disorder

A. Moderate or greater impairment in personality functioning, manifested by characteristic difficulties in two or more of the following four areas:

1. ***Identity***: Markedly impoverished, poorly developed, or unstable self-image, often associated with excessive self-criticism; chronic feelings of emptiness; dissociative states under stress.
2. ***Self-direction***: Instability in goals, aspirations, values, or career plans.
3. ***Empathy***: Compromised ability to recognize the feelings and needs of others associated with interpersonal hypersensitivity (i.e., prone to feel slighted or insulted); perceptions of others selectively biased toward negative attributes or vulnerabilities.
4. ***Intimacy***: Intense, unstable, and conflicted close relationships, marked by mistrust, neediness, and anxious preoccupation with real or imagined abandonment; close relationships often viewed in extremes of idealization and devaluation and alternating between overinvolvement and withdrawal.

B. Four or more of the following seven pathological personality traits, at least one of which must be (5) Impulsivity, (6) Risk taking, or (7) Hostility:

1. **Emotional lability** (an aspect of **Negative Affectivity**): Unstable emotional experiences and frequent mood changes; emotions that

are easily aroused, intense, and/or out of proportion to events and circumstances.

2. **Anxiousness** (an aspect of **Negative Affectivity**): Intense feelings of nervousness, tenseness, or panic, often in reaction to interpersonal stresses; worry about the negative effects of past unpleasant experiences and future negative possibilities; feeling fearful, apprehensive, or threatened by uncertainty; fears of falling apart or losing control.
3. **Separation insecurity** (an aspect of **Negative Affectivity**): Fears of rejection by—and/or separation from—significant others, associated with fears of excessive dependency and complete loss of autonomy.
4. **Depressivity** (as aspect of **Negative Affectivity**): Frequent feelings of being down, miserable, and/or hopeless; difficulty recovering from such moods; pessimism about the future; pervasive shame; feelings of inferior self-worth; thoughts of suicide and suicidal behavior.
5. **Impulsivity** (an aspect of **Disinhibition**): Acting on the spur of the moment in response to immediate stimuli; acting on a momentary basis without a plan or consideration of outcomes; difficulty establishing or following plans; a sense of urgency and self-harming behavior under emotional distress.
6. **Risk taking** (an aspect of **Disinhibition**): Engagement in dangerous, risky, and potentially self-damaging activities, unnecessarily and without regard to consquences; lack of concern for one's limitations and denial of the reality of personal danger.
7. **Hostility** (an aspect of **Antagonism**): Persistent or frequent angry feelings; anger or irritability in response to minor slights and insults.

PROPOSED CLINICIAN-RATED DIMENSIONS OF PSYCHOSIS SYMPTOM SEVERITY

Below you will find an example of one of the "emerging measures", that is, a proposed new DSM-5 rating scale which will be evaluated by researchers and clinicians to determine whether it is a useful instrument to enhance clinical decision-making and to monitor treatment progress.

Clinician-Rated Dimensions of Psychosis Symptom Severity

Name:______________________________ **Age:**______

Sex: [ ] Male [ ] Female **Date:**______________

Instructions: Based on all the information you have on the individual and using your clinical judgment, please rate (with checkmark) the presence and severity of the following symptoms as experience by the individual in the past seven (7) days.

Domain	0	1	2	3	4	Score
I. Hallucinations	□ Not present	□ Equivocal (severity or duration not sufficient to be considered psychosis)	□ Present, but mild (little pressure to act upon voices, not very bothered by voices)	□ Present and moderate (some pressure to respond to voices, or is somewhat bothered by voices)	□ Present and severe (severe pressure to respond to voices, or is very bothered by voices)	
II. Delusions	□ Not present	□ Equivocal (severity or duration not sufficient to be considered psychosis)	□ Present, but mild (little pressure to act upon delusional beliefs, not very bothered by beliefs)	□ Present and moderate (some pressure to act upon beliefs, or is somewhat bothered by beliefs)	□ Present and severe (severe pressure to act upon beliefs, or is very bothered by beliefs)	
III. Disorganized speech	□ Not present	□ Equivocal (severity or duration not sufficient to be considered disorganized)	□ Present, but mild (some difficulty following speech)	□ Present and moderate (speech often difficult to follow)	□ Present and severe (speech almost impossible to follow)	
IV. Abnormal psychomotor behavior	□ Not present	□ Equivocal (severity or duration not sufficient to be considered abnormal psychomotor	□ Present, but mild (occasional abnormal or bizarre motor behavior or catatonia)	□ Present and moderate (frequent abnormal or bizarre motor behavior or catatonia)	□ Present and severe (abnormal or bizarre motor behavior or catatonia almost	

		behavior)			constant)	
V. Negative symptoms (restricted emotional expression or avolition)	□ Not present	□ Equivocal decrease in facial expressivity, prosody, gestures, or self-initiated behavior	□ Present, but mild decrease in facial expressivity, prosody, gestures, or self-initiated behavior	□ Present and moderate decrease in facial expressivity, prosody, gestures, or self-initiated behavior	□ Present and severe decrease in facial expressivity, prosody, gestures, or self-initiated behavior	
VI. Impaired cognition	□ Not present	Equivocal (cognitive function not clearly outside the range expected for age or SES; i.e., within 0.5 SD of mean)	□ Present, but mild (some reduction in cognitive function; below expected for age and SES, 0.5-1 SD from mean)	□ Present and moderate (clear reduction in cognitive function; below expected for age and SES, 1-2 SD from mean)	□ Present and severe (severe reduction in cognitive function; below expected for age and SES, >2 SD from mean)	
VII. Depression	□ Not present	□ Equivocal (Occasionally feels sad, down, depressed, or hopeless; concerned about having failed someone or at something but not preoccupied)	□ Present but mild (frequent periods of feeling very sad, down, moderately depressed, or hopeless; concerned about having failed someone or at something with some pre-occupation)	□ Present and moderate (frequent periods of deep depression or hopelessness; preoccupation with guilt, having done wrong)	□ Present and severe (deeply depressed or hopeless daily; delusional guilt or unreasonable self-reproach grossly out of proportion to circum-stances)	
VIII. Mania	□ Not present	□ Equivocal (occasional elevated, expansive, or irritable mood or some restlessness)	□ Present, but mild (frequent periods of somewhat elevated, expansive, or irritable mood or restlessness)	□ Present and moderate (frequent periods of extensively elevated, expansive, or irritable mood or restlessness)	□ Present and severe (daily and extensively elevated, expansive, or irritable mood or restlessness)	

Note. SD=standard deviation; SES=socio-economic status.

DIAGNOSTIC CRITERIA FOR SELECTED DSM-5 DISORDERS

While the overview of diagnostic classifications provided a "big picture" of mental health conditions, the diagnostic criteria give us "fine grain" details of specific disorders. It is the task of the mental health diagnostician to determine whether the person who is being evaluated meets the diagnostic criteria in order to identify what kind of disorder might be accounting for the particular cluster of symptoms that he or she is experiencing. Below you will find selected disorders and the main criteria that are used by diagnosticians in their clinical practices and scientific research.

Diagnostic Criteria for Panic Disorder

A. Recurrent unexpected panic attacks. A panic attack is an abrupt surge of intense fear or intense discomfort that reaches a peak within minutes, and during which time four (or more) of the following symptoms occur:

1. Palpitations, pounding heart or accelerated heart rate.
2. Sweating.
3. Trembling or shaking.
4. Sensations of shortness of breath or smothering.
5. Feelings of choking.
6. Chest pain or discomfort.
7. Nausea or abdominal distress.
8. Feeling dizzy, unsteady, light-headed or faint.
9. Chills or heat sensations.
10. Parathesias (numbness or tingling sensations).
11. Derealization (feelings of unreality) or depersonalization (being detached from oneself).
12. Fear of losing control or "going crazy".
13. Fear of dying.

B. At least one of the attacks has been accompanied by one month (or more) of one or both of the following:

1. Persistent concern or worry about additional panic attacks or their consequences (e.g., losing control, having a heart attack, "going crazy").
2. A significant maladaptive change in behavior related to the attacks (e.g., behaviors designed to avoid having panic attacks, such as avoidance of exercise or unfamiliar situations).

C. The disturbance is not attributable to the physiological effects of a substance (e.g., a drug of abuse, a medication) or other medical condition (e.g., hyperthyroidism, cardiopulmonary disorders).

D. The disturbance is not better explained by another mental disorder (e.g., the panic attacks do not occur only in response to feared social situations, as in social anxiety disorder; in response to circumscribed phobic objects or situations, as in specific phobia; in response to obsessions, as in obsessive-compulsive disorder; in response to reminders of traumatic events, as in posttraumatic stress disorder; or in response to separation from attachment figures, as in separation anxiety disorder).

Diagnostic Criteria for Agoraphobia

A. Marked fear or anxiety about two (or more) of the following five situations:
   1. Using public transportation (e.g., automobiles, buses, trains, ships, planes).
   2. Being in open spaces (e.g., parking lots, marketplaces, bridges).
   3. Being in enclosed places (e.g., shops, theaters, cinemas).
   4. Standing in line or being in a crowd.
   5. Being outside of the home alone.

B. The individual fears or avoids these situations because of thoughts that escape might be difficult or help might not be available in the event of developing panic-like symptoms or other incapacitating or embarrassing symptoms (e.g., fear of falling in the elderly; fear of incontinence).

C. The agoraphobic situations almost always provoke fear or anxiety.

D. The agoraphobic situations are actively avoided, require the presence of a companion, or are endured with intense fear or anxiety.

E. The fear or anxiety is out of proportion to the actual danger posed by the agoraphobic situations and to the sociocultural context.

F. The fear, anxiety, or avoidance is persistent, typically lasting for 6 months or more.

G. The fear, anxiety, or avoidance causes clinically significant distress or impairment in social, occupational, or other important areas of functioning.

H. If another medical condition (e.g., inflammatory bowel disease, Parkinson's disease) is present, the fear, anxiety, or avoidance is clearly excessive.

I. The fear, anxiety, or avoidance is not better explained by the symptoms of another mental disorder—for example, the symptoms are not confined to specific phobia, situational type; do not involve only social situations (as in social anxiety disorder); and are not related exclusively to obsessions (as in obsessive-compulsive disorder), perceived defects or flaws in physical appearance (as in body dysmorphic disorder), reminders of traumatic events (as in posttraumatic stress disorder), or fear of separation (as in separation anxiety disorder).

Note: Agoraphobia is diagnosed irrespective of the presence of panic disorder. If an individual's presentation meets criteria for panic disorder and agoraphobia, both diagnoses should be assigned.

Diagnostic Criteria for Posttraumatic Stress Disorder

A. Exposure to actual or threatened death, serious injury, or sexual violence in one (or more) of the following ways:

1. Directly experiencing the traumatic event(s).
2. Witnessing, in person, the event(s) as it occurred to others.
3. Learning that the traumatic event(s) occurred to a close family member or close friend. In cases of actual or threatened death of a family member or friend, the event(s) must have been violent or accidental.
4. Experiencing repeated or extreme exposure to aversive details of the traumatic event(s) (e.g., first responders collecting human remains; police officers repeatedly exposed to details of child abuse).

Note: Criterion A4 does not apply to exposure through electronic media, television, movies, or pictures, unless this exposure is work related.

B. Presence of one (or more) of the following intrusion symptoms associated with the traumatic event(s), beginning after the traumatic event(s) occurred:

1. Recurrent, involuntary, and intrusive distressing memories of the traumatic event(s).

2. Recurrent distressing dreams in which the content and/or affect of the dream are related to the traumatic event(s).
3. Dissociative reactions (e.g., flashbacks) in which the individual feels or acts as if the traumatic event(s) were recurring. (Such reactions may occur on a continuum, with the most extreme expression being a complete loss of awareness of present surroundings.)
4. Intense or prolonged psychological distress at exposure to internal or external cues that symbolize or resemble an aspect of the traumatic event(s).
5. Marked physiological reactions to internal or external cues that symbolize or resemble an aspect of the traumatic event(s).

C. Persistent avoidance of stimuli associated with the traumatic event(s), beginning after the traumatic event(s) occurred, as evidenced by one or both of the following:

1. Avoidance of or efforts to avoid distressing memories, thoughts, or feelings about or closely associated with the traumatic event(s).
2. Avoidance of or efforts to avoid external reminders (people, places, conversations, activities, objects, situations) that arouse distressing memories, thoughts, or feelings about or closely associated with the traumatic event(s).

D. Negative alternations in cognitions and mood associated with the traumatic event(s) beginning or worsening after the traumatic event(s) occurred, as evidenced by two (or more) of the following:

1. Inability to remember an important aspect of the traumatic event(s) (typically due to dissociative amnesia and not to other factors such as head injury, alcohol, or drugs).
2. Persistent and exaggerated negative beliefs or expectations about oneself, others, or the world (e.g., "I am bad," "No one can be trusted," "The world is completely dangerous," "My whole nervous system is permanently ruined").
3. Persistent, distorted cognitions about the cause or consequences of the traumatic event(s) that lead the individual to blame himself/herself or others.
4. Persistent negative emotional state (e.g., fear, horror, anger, guilt, or shame).
5. Markedly diminished interest or participation in significant activities.
6. Feelings of detachment or estrangement from others.
7. Persistent inability to experience positive emotions (e.g., inability to experience happiness, satisfaction, or loving feelings).

E. Marked alterations in arousal and reactivity associated with the traumatic event(s), beginning or worsening after the traumatic event(s) occurred, as evidenced by two (or more) of the following:
   1. Irritable behavior and angry outbursts (with little or no provocation) typically expressed as verbal or physical aggression toward people or objects.
   2. Reckless or self-destructive behavior.
   3. Hypervigilance.
   4. Exaggerated startle response.
   5. Problems with concentration.
   6. Sleep disturbance (e.g., difficulty falling or staying asleep or restless sleep).

F. Duration of the disturbance (Criteria B, C, D, and E) is more than 1 month.

G. The disturbance causes clinically significant distress or impairment in social, occupational, or other important areas of functioning.

H. The disturbance is not attributable to the physiological effects of a substance (e.g., medication, alcohol) or another medical condition.

Specify whether:

With dissociative symptoms: The individual's symptoms meet the criteria for post-traumatic stress disorder, and in addition, in response to the stressor, the individual experiences persistent or recurrent symptoms of either of the following:

1. **Depersonalization**: Persistent or recurrent experiences of feeling detached from, and as if one were an outside observer of, one's mental processes or body (e.g., feeling as though one were in a dream; feeling a sense of unreality of self or body or of time moving slowly).
2. **Derealization:** Persistent or recurrent experiences of unreality of surroundings (e.g., the world around the individual is experienced as unreal, dreamlike, distant, or distorted).

Note: To use this subtype, the dissociative symptoms must not be attributable to the physiological effects of a substance (e.g., blackouts, behavior during alcohol intoxication) or another medical condition (e.g., complex partial seizures).

Specify if:

With delayed expression: if the full diagnostic criteria are not met until at least 6 months after the event (although the onset and expression of some symptoms may be immediate).

Diagnostic Criteria for Somatic Symptom Disorder

A. One or more somatic symptoms that are distressing or result in significant disruption of daily life.

B. Excessive thoughts, feelings, or behaviors related to the somatic symptoms or associated health concerns as manifested by at least one of the following:
   1. Disproportionate and persistent thoughts about the seriousness of one's symptoms.
   2. Persistently high level of anxiety about health or symptoms.
   3. Excessive time and energy devoted to these symptoms or health concerns.

C. Although any one somatic symptom may not be continuously present, the state of being symptomatic is persistent (typically more than 6 months).

Specify if:

With predominant pain (previously pain disorder): This specifier is for individuals whose somatic symptoms predominantly involve pain.

Specify if:

Persistent: A persistent course is characterized by severe symptoms, marked impairment, and long duration (more than 6 months).

Diagnostic Criteria for Dissociative Identity Disorder

A. Disruption of identity characterized by two or more distinct personality states, which may be described in some cultures as an experience of possession. The disruption in identity involves marked discontinuity in sense of self and sense of agency, accompanied by related alterations in affect, behavior, consciousness, memory, perception, cognition, and/or sensory-motor functioning. These signs and symptoms may be observed by others or reported by the individual.

B. Recurrent gaps in the recall of everyday events, important personal information, and/or traumatic events that are inconsistent with ordinary forgetting.

C. The symptoms cause clinically significant distress or impairment in social, occupational, or other important areas of functioning.

D. The disturbance is not a normal part of a broadly accepted cultural or religious practice.

Note: In children, the symptoms are not better explained by imaginary playmates or other fantasy play.

E. The symptoms are not attributable to the physiological effects of a substance (e.g., blackouts or chaotic behavior during alcohol intoxication) or another medical condition (e.g., complex partial seizures).

Diagnostic Criteria for Anorexia Nervosa

A. Restriction of energy intake relative to requirements, leading to a significantly low body weight in the context of age, sex, developmental trajectory, and physical health. *Significantly low weight* is defined as a weight that is less than minimally normal or, for children and adolescents, less than that minimally expected.

B. Intense fear of gaining weight or of becoming fat, or persistent behavior that interferes with weight gain, even though at a significantly low weight.

C. Disturbance in the way in which one's body weight or shape is experienced, undue influence of body weight or shape on self-evaluation, or persistent lack of recognition of the seriousness of the current low body weight.

Specify whether:

Restricting type: During the last 3 months, the individual has not engaged in recurrent episodes of binge eating or purging behavior (i.e., self-induced vomiting or the misuse of laxatives, diuretics, or enemas). This subtype describes presentations in which weight loss is accomplished primarily through dieting, fasting, and/or excessive exercise.
Binge-eating/purging type: During the last 3 months, the individual has engaged in recurrent episodes of binge eating or purging behavior (i.e., self-induced vomiting or the misuse of laxatives, diuretics, or enemas).

Specify if:

In partial remission: After full criteria for anorexia nervosa were previously met, Criterion A (low body weight) has not been met for a sustained period, but either Criterion B (intense fear of gaining weight or becoming fat or behavior that interferes with weight gain) or Criterion C (disturbances in self-perception of weight and shape) is still met.
In full remission: After full criteria for anorexia nervosa were previously met, none of the criteria have been met for a sustained period of time.

Specify current severity:

The minimum level of severity is based, for adults, on current body mass index (BMI) (see below) or, for children and adolescents, on BMI percentile. The ranges below are derived from World Health Organization categories for thinness in adults; for children and adolescents, corresponding BMI percentiles should be used. The level of severity may be increased to reflect clinical symptoms, the degree of functional disability, and the need for supervision.

Mild: BMI $\geq$ 17 kg/m^2
Moderate: BMI 16-16.99 kg/m^2
Severe: BMI 15-15.99 kg/m^2
Extreme: BMI < kg/m^2

Diagnostic Criteria for Bulimia Nervosa

A. Recurrent episodes of binge eating. An episode of binge eating is characterized by both of the following:
   1. Eating, in a discrete period of time (e.g., within any 2-hour period), an amount of food that is definitely larger than what most individuals would eat in a similar period of time under similar circumstances.
   2. A sense of lack of control over eating during the episode (e.g., a feeling that one cannot stop eating or control what or how much one is eating).

B. Recurrent inappropriate compensatory behaviors in order to prevent weight gain, such as self-induced vomiting; misuse of laxatives, diuretics, or other medications; fasting; or excessive exercise.

C. The binge eating and inappropriate compensatory behaviors both occur, on average, at least once a week for 3 months.

D. Self-evaluation is unduly influenced by body shape and weight.

E. The disturbance does not occur exclusively during episodes of anorexia nervosa.

Specify if:

In partial remission: After full criteria for bulimia nervosa were previously met, some, but not all, of the criteria have been met for a sustained period of time.
In full remission: After full criteria for bulimia nervosa were previously met, none of the criteria have been met for a sustained period of time.

Specify current severity:

The minimum level of severity is based on the frequency of inappropriate compensatory behaviors (see below). The level of severity may be increased to reflect other symptoms and the degree of functional disability.

Mild: An average of 1-3 episodes of inappropriate compensatory behaviors per week.
Moderate: An average of 4-7 episodes of inappropriate compensatory behaviors per week.
Severe: An average of 8-13 episodes of inappropriate compensatory behaviors per week.
Extreme: An average of 14 or more episodes of inappropriate compensatory behaviors per week.

Diagnostic Criteria for Major Depressive Disorder

A. Five (or more) of the following symptoms have been present during the same 2-week period and represent a change from previous functioning; at least one of the symptoms is either (1) depressed mood or (2) loss of interest or pleasure.

Note: Do not include symptoms that are clearly attributable to another medical condition.

1. Depressed mood most of the day, nearly every day, as indicated by either subjective report (e.g., feels sad, empty, hopeless) or observation made by others (e.g., appears tearful). (**Note:** In children and adolescents, can be irritable mood.)
2. Markedly diminished interest or pleasure in all, or almost all, activities most of the day, nearly every day (as indicated by either subjective account or observation).
3. Significant weight loss when not dieting or weight gain (e.g., a change of more than 5% of body weight in a month), or decrease or increase in appetite nearly every day. (**Note:** In children, consider failure to make expected weight gain.)
4. Insomnia or hypersomnia nearly every day.
5. Psychomotor agitation or retardation nearly every day (observable by others, not merely subjective feelings of restlessness or being slowed down).
6. Fatigue or loss of energy nearly every day.
7. Feelings of worthlessness or excessive or inappropriate guilt (which may be delusional) nearly every day (not merely self-reproach or guilt about being sick).

8. Diminished ability to think or concentrate, or indecisiveness, nearly every day (either by subjective account or as observed by others).
9. Recurrent thoughts of death (not just fear of dying), recurrent suicidal ideation without a specific plan, or a suicide attempt or a specific plan for committing suicide.

B. The symptoms cause clinically significant distress or impairment in social, occupational, or other important areas of functioning.

C. The episode is not attributable to the physiological effects of a substance or to another medical condition.

Note: Criteria A-C represent a major depressive episode.

Note: Responses to a significant loss (e.g., bereavement, financial ruin, losses from a natural disaster, a serious medical illness or disability) may include the feelings of intense sadness, rumination about the loss, insomnia, poor appetite, and weight loss noted in Criterion A, which may resemble a depressive episode. Although such symptoms may be understandable or considered appropriate to the loss, the presence of a major depressive episode in addition to the normal response to a significant loss should also be carefully considered. This decision inevitably requires the exercise of clinical judgment based on the individual's history and the cultural norms for the expression of distress in the context of loss.[1]

D. The occurrence of the major depressive episode is not better explained by schizoaffective disorder, schizophrenia, schizophreniform disorder, delusional disorder, or other specified and unspecified schizophrenia spectrum and other psychotic disorders.

---

[1] In distinguishing grief from a major depressive episode (MDE), it is useful to consider that in grief the predominant affect is feelings of emptiness and loss, while in MDE it is persistent depressed mood and the inability to anticipate happiness or pleasure. The dysphoria in grief is likely to decrease in intensity over days to weeks and occurs in waves, the so-called pangs of grief. These waves tend to be associated with thoughts or reminders of the deceased. The depressed mood of MDE is more persistent and not tied to specific thoughts or preoccupations. The pain of grief may be accompanied by positive emotions and humor that are uncharacteristic of the pervasive unhappiness and misery characteristic of MDE. The thought content associated with grief generally features a preoccupation with thoughts and memories of the deceased, rather than the self-critical or pessimistic ruminations seen in MDE. In grief, self-esteem is generally preserved, whereas in MDE feelings of worthlessness and self-loathing are common. If self-derogatory ideation is present in grief, it typically involves perceived failings vis-à-vis the deceased (e.g., not visiting frequently enough, not telling the deceased how much he or she was loved). If a bereaved individual thinks about death and dying, such as thoughts are generally focused on the deceased and possibly about "joining" the deceased, whereas in MDE such thoughts are focused on ending one's own life because of feeling worthless, undeserving of life, or unable to cope with the pain of depression.

E. There has never been a manic episode or a hypomanic episode.

Note: This exclusion does not apply if all of the manic-like or hypomanic-like episodes are substance-induced or are attributable to the physiological effects of another medical condition.

In recording the name of a diagnosis, terms should be listed in the following order; major depressive disorder, single or recurrent episode, severity/psychotic/remission specifiers, followed by as many of the following specifiers without codes that apply to the current episode.

Specify:
With anxious distress
With mixed features
With melancholic features
With atypical features
With mood-congruent psychotic features
With mood-incongruent psychotic features
With catatonia
With peripartum onset
With seasonal pattern

Diagnostic Criteria for Bipolar I Disorder

Manic Episode

A. A distinct period of abnormally and persistently elevated, expansive, or irritable mood and abnormally and persistently increased goal-directed activity or energy, lasting at least 1 week and present most of the day, nearly every day (or any duration if hospitalization is necessary).

B. During the period of mood disturbance and increased energy or activity, three (or more) of the following symptoms (four if the mood is only irritable) are present to a significant degree and represent a noticeable change from usual behavior:

1. Inflated self-esteem or grandiosity.
2. Decreased need for sleep (e.g., feels rested after only 3 hours of sleep).
3. More talkative than usual or pressure to keep talking.
4. Flight of ideas for subjective experience that thoughts are racing.
5. Distractibility (i.e., attention too easily drawn to unimportant or irrelevant external stimuli), as reported or observed.
6. Increase in goal-directed activity (either social, at work or school, or sexually) or psychomotor agitation (i.e., purposeless non-goal-directed activity).

7. Excessive involvement in activities that have a high potential for painful consequences (e.g., engaging in unrestrained buying sprees, sexual indiscretions, or foolish business investments).

C. The mood disturbance is sufficiently severe to cause marked impairment in social or occupational functioning or to necessitate hospitalization to prevent harm to self or others, or there are psychotic features.

D. The episode is not attributable to the physiological effects of a substance (e.g., a drug of abuse, a medication, other treatment) or to another medical condition.

Note: A full manic episode that emerges during antidepressant treatment (e.g., medication, electroconvulsive therapy) but persists at a fully syndromal level beyond the physiological effect of that treatment is sufficient evidence for a manic episode and, therefore, a bipolar I diagnosis.

Note: Criteria A-D constitute a manic episode. At least one lifetime manic episode is required for the diagnosis of bipolar I disorder.

Hypomanic Episode

A. A distinct period of abnormally and persistently elevated, expansive, or irritable mood and abnormally and persistently increased activity or energy, lasting at least 4 consecutive dates and present most of the day, nearly every day.

B. During the period of mood disturbance and increased energy and activity, three (or more) of the following symptoms (four if the mood is only irritable) have persisted, represent a noticeable change from usual behavior, and have been present to a significant degree:

1. Inflated self-esteem or grandiosity.
2. Decreased need for sleep (e.g., feels rested after only 3 hours of sleep).
3. More talkative than usual or pressure to keep talking.
4. Flight of ideas or subjective experience that thoughts are racing.
5. Distractibility (i.e., attention too easily drawn to unimportant or irrelevant external stimuli), as reported or observed.
6. Increase in goal-directed activity (either socially, at work or school, or sexually) or psychomotor agitation.
7. Excessive involvement in activities that have a high potential for painful consequences (e.g., engaging in unrestrained buying sprees, sexual indiscretions, or foolish business investments).

C. The episode is associated with an unequivocal change in functioning that is uncharacteristic of the individual when not symptomatic.

D. The disturbance in mood and the change in functioning are observable by others.

E. The episode is not severe enough to cause marked impairment in social or occupational functioning or to necessitate hospitalization. If there are psychotic feature, the episode is, by definition, manic.

F. The episode is not attributable to the physiological effects of a substance (e.g., a drug of abuse, a medication, other treatment).

Note: A full hypomanic episode that emerges during antidepressant treatment (e.g., medication, electroconvulsive therapy) but persists at a fully syndromal level beyond the physiological effect of that treatment is sufficient evidence for a hypomanic episode diagnosis. However, caution is indicated so that one or two symptoms (particularly increased irritability, edginess, or agitation following antidepressant use) are not taken as sufficient for diagnosis of a hypomanic episode, nor necessarily indicative or a bipolar diathesis.

Note: Criteria A-F constitute a hypomanic episode. Hypomanic episodes are common in bipolar I disorder but are not required for the diagnosis of bipolar I disorder.

Major Depressive Episode

A. Five (or more) of the following symptoms have been present during the same 2-week period and represent a change from previous functioning; at least one of the symptoms is either (1) depressed mood or (2) loss of interest or pleasure.

Note: Do not include symptoms that are clearly attributable to another medical condition.

1. Depressed mood most of the day, nearly every day, as indicated by either subjective report (e.g., feels sad, empty, or hopeless) or observation made by other (e.g., appears tearful). (**Note:** In children and adolescents, can be irritable mood.)
2. Markedly diminished interest or pleasure in all, or almost all, activities most of the day, nearly every day (as indicated by either subjective account or observation).
3. Significant weight loss when not dieting or weight gain (e.g., a change of more than 5% of body weight in a month), or decrease or increase in appetite nearly every day. (**Note:** In children, consider failure to make expected weight gain.)
4. Insomnia or hypersomnia nearly every day.
5. Psychomotor agitation or retardation nearly every day (observable by others; not merely subjective feelings of restlessness or being slowed down).

6. Fatigue or loss of energy nearly every day.
7. Feelings of worthlessness or excessive or inappropriate guilt (which may be delusional) nearly every day (not merely self-reproach or guilt about being sick).
8. Diminished ability to think or concentrate, or indecisiveness, nearly every day (either by subjective account or as observed by others).
9. Recurrent thoughts of death (not just fear of dying), recurrent suicidal ideation without a specific plan, or a suicide attempt or a specific plan for committing suicide.

B. The symptoms cause clinically significant distress or impairment in social, occupational, or other important areas of functioning.

C. The episode is not attributable to the physiological effects of a substance or another medical condition.

Note: Criteria A-C constitute a major depressive episode. Major depressive episodes are common in bipolar I disorder but are not required for the diagnosis of bipolar I disorder.

Bipolar I Disorder

A. Criteria have been met for at least one manic episode (Criteria A-D under "Manic Episode" above).

B. The occurrence of the manic and major depressive episode(s) is not better explained by schizoaffective disorder, schizophrenia, schizophreniform disorder, delusional disorder, or other specified or unspecified schizophrenia spectrum and other psychotic disorder.

In recording the name of a diagnosis, terms should be listed in the following order: bipolar I disorder, type of current or most recent episode, severity/psychotic/remission specifiers, followed by as many specifiers without codes as apply to the current or most recent episode.

Specify:

With anxious distress
With mixed features
With rapid cycling
With melancholic features
With atypical features
With mood-congruent psychotic features
With mood-incongruent psychotic features
With catatonia
With peripartum onset
With seasonal pattern

Diagnostic Criteria for Schizophrenia

A. Two (or more) of the following, each present for a significant portion of time during a 1-month period (or less if successfully treated). At least one of these must be (1), (2), or (3):
   1. Delusions.
   2. Hallucinations.
   3. Disorganized speech (e.g., frequent derailment or incoherence).
   4. Grossly disorganized or catatonic behavior.
   5. Negative symptoms (i.e., diminished emotional expression or avolition).

B. For a significant portion of the time since the onset of the disturbance, level of functioning in one or more major areas, such as work, interpersonal relations, or self-care, is markedly below the level achieved prior to the onset (or when the onset is in the childhood or adolescence, there is failure to achieve expected level of interpersonal, academic, or occupational functioning).

C. Continuous signs of the disturbance persist for at least 6 months. This 6-month period must include at least 1 month of symptoms (or less if successfully treated) that meet Criterion A (i.e., active-phase symptoms) and may include periods of prodromal or residual symptoms. During these prodromal or residual periods, the signs of the disturbance may be manifested by only negative symptoms or by two or more symptoms listed in Criterion A present in an attenuated form (e.g., odd beliefs, unusual perceptual experiences).

D. Schizoaffective disorder and depressive or bipolar disorder with psychotic features have been ruled out because either 1) no major depressive or manic episodes have occurred concurrently with the active-phase symptoms, or 2) if mood episodes have occurred during active-phase symptoms, they have been present for a minority of the total duration of the active and residual periods of the illness.

E. The disturbance is not attributable to the physiological effects of a substance (e.g., a drug of abuse, a medication) or another medical condition.

F. If there is a history of autism spectrum disorder or a communication disorder of childhood onset, the additional diagnosis of schizophrenia is made only if prominent delusions or hallucinations, in addition to the other required symptoms of schizophrenia, are also present for at least 1 month (or less if successfully treated).

Specify if:

The following course specifiers are only to be used after a 1-year duration of the disorder and if they are not in contradiction to the diagnostic course criteria.

First episode, currently in acute episode: First manifestation of the disorder meeting the defining diagnostic symptom and time criteria. An *acute episode* is a time period in which the symptom criteria are fulfilled.
First episode, currently in partial remission: *Partial remission* is a period of time during which an improvement after a previous episode is maintained and in which the defining criteria of the disorder are only partially fulfilled.
First episode, currently in full remission: *Full remission* is a period of time after a previous episode during which no disorder-specific symptoms are present.
Multiple episodes, currently in acute episode: Multiple episodes may be determined after a minimum of two episodes (i.e., after a first episode, a remission and a minimum of one relapse).
Multiple episodes, currently in partial remission
Multiple episodes, currently in full remission
Continuous: Symptoms fulfilling the diagnostic *symptom* criteria of the disorder are remaining for the majority of the illness course, with subthreshold symptom periods being very brief relative to the overall course.
Unspecified

Specify if:

With catatonia

Specify current severity:

Severity is rated by a quantitative assessment of the primary symptoms of psychosis, including delusions, hallucinations, disorganized speech, abnormal psychomotor behavior, and negative symptoms. Each of these symptoms may be rated for its current severity (most severe in the last 7 days) on a 5-point scale ranging from 0 (not present) to 4 (present and severe). (See Clinician-Rated Dimensions of Psychosis Symptom Severity in the chapter “Assessment Measures”.)

Note: Diagnosis of schizophrenia can be made without using this severity specifier.

Diagnostic Criteria for Delusional Disorder

A. The presence of one (or more) delusions with a duration of 1 month or longer.

B. Criterion A for schizophrenia has never been met.

Note: Hallucinations, if present, are not prominent and are related to the delusional theme (e.g., the sensation of being infested with insects associated with delusions of infestation).

C. Apart from the impact of the delusion(s) or its ramifications, functioning is not markedly impaired, and behavior is not obviously bizarre or odd.

D. If manic or major depressive episodes have occurred, these have been brief relative to the duration of the delusional periods.

E. The disturbance is not attributable to the physiological effects of a substance or another medical condition and is not better explained by another mental disorder, such as body dysmorphic disorder or obsessive-compulsive disorder.

Specify whether:

Erotomanic type: This subtype applies when the central theme of the delusion is that another person is in love with the individual.
Grandiose type: This subtype applies when the central theme of the delusion is the conviction of having some great (but unrecognized) talent or insight or having made some important discovery.
Jealous type: This subtype applies when the central theme of the individual's delusion is that his or her spouse or lover is unfaithful.
Persecutory type: This subtype applies when the central theme of the delusion involves the individual's belief that he or she is being conspired against, cheated, spied on, followed, poisoned or drugged, maliciously maligned, harassed, or obstructed in the pursuit of long-term goals.
Somatic type: This subtype applies when the central theme of the delusion involves bodily functions or sensations.
Mixed type: This subtype applies when no one delusional theme predominates.
Unspecified type: This subtype applies when the dominant delusional belief cannot be clearly determined or is not described in the specific types (e.g., referential delusions without a prominent persecutory or grandiose component).

Specify if:

With bizarre content: Delusions are deemed bizarre if they are clearly implausible, not understandable, and not derived from ordinary life experiences (e.g., an individual's belief that a stranger has removed his or her internal organs and replaced them with someone else's organs without leaving any wounds or scars.

Diagnostic Criteria for Alcohol Use Disorder

A. A problematic pattern of alcohol use leading to clinically significant impairment or distress, as manifested by at least two of the following, occurring within a 12-month period:

1. Alcohol is often taken in larger amounts or over a longer period than was intended.
2. There is a persistent desire or unsuccessful efforts to cut down or control alcohol use.
3. A great deal of time is spent in activities necessary to obtain alcohol, use alcohol, or recover from its effects.
4. Craving, or a strong desire or urge to use alcohol.
5. Recurrent alcohol use resulting in a failure to fulfill major role obligations at work, school, or home.
6. Continued alcohol use despite having persistent or recurrent social or interpersonal problems caused or exacerbated by the effects of alcohol.
7. Important social, occupational, or recreational activities are given up or reduced because of alcohol use.
8. Recurrent alcohol use in situations in which it is physically hazardous.
9. Alcohol use is continued despite knowledge of having a persistent or recurrent physical or psychological problem that is likely to have been caused or exacerbated by alcohol.
10. Tolerance, as defined by either of the following:
    a. A need for markedly increased amounts of alcohol to achieve intoxication or desired effect.
    b. A markedly diminished effect with continued use of the same amount of alcohol.
11. Withdrawal, as manifested by either of the following:
    a. The characteristic withdrawal syndrome for alcohol.
    b. Alcohol (or a closely related substance, such as a benzodiazepine) is taken to relieve or avoid withdrawal symptoms.

Specify if:

In early remission: After full criteria for alcohol use disorder were previously met, none of the criteria for alcohol use disorder have been met for at least 3 months but for less than 12 months (with the exception that Criterion A4, “Craving, or a strong desire or urge to use alcohol,” may be met).

In sustained remission: After full criteria for alcohol use disorder were previously met, none of the criteria for alcohol use disorder have been met at any time during a period of 12 months or longer (with the exception that Criterion A4, "Craving, or a strong desire or urge to use alcohol," may be met).

Specify if:

In a controlled environment: This additional specifier is used if the individual is in an environment where access to alcohol is restricted.

Specify current severity:

Mild: Presence of 2-3 symptoms.
Moderate: Presence of 4-5 symptoms.
Severe: Presence of 6 or more symptoms.

Diagnostic Criteria for Alcohol Intoxication

A. Recent ingestion of alcohol.
B. Clinically significant problematic behavioral or psychological changes (e.g., inappropriate sexual or aggressive behavior, mood lability, impaired judgment) that developed during, or shortly after, alcohol ingestion.
C. One (or more) of the following signs or symptoms developing during, or shortly after, alcohol use:
   1. Slurred speech.
   2. Incoordination.
   3. Unsteady gait.
   4. Nystagmus.
   5. Impairment in attention or memory.
   6. Stupor or coma.
D. The signs or symptoms are not attributable to another medical condition and are not better explained by another mental disorder, including intoxication with another substance.

Diagnostic Criteria for Alcohol Withdrawal

A. Cessation of (or reduction in) alcohol use that has been heavy and prolonged.
B. Two (or more) of the following, developing within several hours to a few days after the cessation of (or reduction in) alcohol use described in Criterion A:

1. Autonomic hyperactivity (e.g., sweating or pulse rate greater than 100 bpm).
2. Increased hand tremor.
3. Insomnia.
4. Nausea or vomiting.
5. Transient visual, tactile, or auditory hallucinations or illusions.
6. Psychomotor agitation.
7. Anxiety.
8. Generalized tonic-clonic seizures.

C. The signs or symptoms in Criterion B cause clinically significant distress or impairment in social, occupational, or other important areas of functioning.

D. The signs or symptoms are not attributable to another medical condition and are not better explained by another mental disorder, including intoxication or withdrawal from another substance.

Specify if:

With perceptual disturbances: This specifier applies in the rare instance when hallucinations (usually visual or tactile) occur with intact reality testing, or auditory, visual, or tactile illusions occur in the absence of a delirium.

Diagnostic Criteria for Cannabis Use Disorder

A. A problematic pattern of cannabis use leading to clinically significant impairment or distress, as manifested by at least two of the following, occurring within a 12-month period:

1. Cannabis is often taken in larger amounts or over a longer period that was intended.
2. There is a persistent desire or unsuccessful efforts to cut down or control cannabis use.
3. A great deal of time is spent in activities necessary to obtain cannabis, use cannabis, or recover from its effects.
4. Craving, or a strong desire or urge to use cannabis.
5. Recurrent cannabis use resulting in a failure to fulfill major role obligations at work, school, or home.
6. Continued cannabis use despite having persistent or recurrent social or interpersonal problems caused or exacerbated by the effects of cannabis.
7. Important social, occupational, or recreational activities that are given up or reduced because of cannabis use.

8. Recurrent cannabis use in situations in which it is physically hazardous.
9. Cannabis use is continued despite knowledge of having a persistent or recurrent physical or psychological problem that is likely to have been caused or exacerbated by cannabis.
10. Tolerance, as defined by either of the following:
    a. A need for markedly increased amounts of cannabis to achieve intoxication or desired effect.
    b. Markedly diminished effect with continued use of the same amount of cannabis.
11. Withdrawal, as manifested by either of the following:
    a. The characteristic withdrawal syndrome for cannabis.
    b. Cannabis (or a closely related substance) is taken to relieve or avoid withdrawal symptoms.

Specify if:

In early remission: After full criteria for cannabis use disorder were previously met, none of the criteria for cannabis use disorder have been met for at least 3 months but for less than 12 months (with the exception that Criterion A4, "Craving, or a strong desire or urge to use cannabis," may be met).
In sustained remission: After full criteria for cannabis use disorder were previously met, none of the criteria for cannabis use disorder have been met at any time during a period of 12 months or longer (with the exception that Criterion A4, "Craving, or a strong desire or urge to use cannabis," may be present).

Specify if:

In a controlled environment: This additional specifier is used if the individual is in an environment where access to cannabis is restricted.

Specify current severity:

Mild: Presence of 2-3 symptoms.
Moderate: Presence of 4-5 symptoms.
Severe: Presence of 6 or more symptoms.

Diagnostic Criteria for Pedophilic Disorder

A. Over a period of at least 6 months, recurrent, intense sexually arousing fantasies, sexual urges, or behaviors involving sexual activity with a prepubescent child or children (generally age 13 years or younger).
B. The individual has acted on these sexual urges, or the sexual urges or fantasies cause marked distress or interpersonal difficulty.

C. The individual is at least age 16 years and at least 5 years older than the child or children in Criterion A.

Note: Do not include an individual in late adolescence involved in an ongoing sexual relationship with a 12- or 13-year-old.

Specify whether:

Exclusive type (attracted only to children)
Nonexclusive type

Specify if:

Sexually attracted to males
Sexually attracted to females
Sexually attracted to both

Specify if:

Limited to incest

Diagnostic Criteria for Gender Dysphoria

Gender Dysphoria in Adolescents and Adults

A. A marked incongruence between one's experience/expressed gender and assigned gender, of at least 6 months' duration, as manifested by at least two of the following:

1. A marked incongruence between one's experienced/expressed gender and primary and/or secondary sex characteristics (or in young adolescents, the anticipated secondary sex characteristics).
2. A strong desire to be rid of one's primary and/or secondary sex characteristics because of a marked incongruence with one's experienced/expressed gender (or in young adolescents, a desire to prevent the development of the anticipated secondary sex characteristics).
3. A strong desire for the primary and/or secondary sex characteristics of the other gender.
4. A strong desire to be of the other gender (or some alternative gender different from one's assigned gender).
5. A strong desire to be treated as the other gender (or some alternative gender different from one's assigned gender).
6. A strong conviction that one has the typical feelings and reactions of the other gender (or some alternative gender different from one's assigned gender).

B. The condition is associated with clinically significant distress or impairment in social, occupational, or other important areas of functioning.

Specify if:

With a disorder of sex development (e.g., a congenital adrenogenital disorder such as congenital adrenal hyperplasia or androgen insensitivity syndrome).

Specify if:

Posttransition: The individual has transitioned to full-time living in the desired gender (with or without legalization of gender change) and has undergone (or is preparing to have) at least one cross-sex medical procedure or treatment regimen—namely, regular cross-sex hormone treatment or gender reassignment surgery confirming the desired gender (e.g., penectomy, vaginoplasty in a natal male; mastectomy or phalloplasty in a natal female).

Diagnostic Criteria for Intellectual Disability (Intellectual Developmental Disorder)

Intellectual disability (intellectual developmental disorder) is a disorder with onset during the developmental period that includes both intellectual and adaptive functioning deficits in conceptual, social, and practical domains. The following three criteria must be met:

A. Deficits in intellectual functions, such as reasoning, problem solving, planning, abstract thinking, judgment, academic learning, and learning from experience, confirmed by both clinical assessment and individualized, standardized intelligence testing.

B. Deficits in adaptive functioning that result in failure to meet developmental and socio-cultural standards for personal independence and social responsibility. Without ongoing support, the adaptive deficits limit functioning in one or more activities of daily life, such as communication, social participation, and independent living, across multiple environments, such as home, school, work, and community.

C. Onset of intellectual and adaptive deficits during the developmental period.

Note: The diagnostic term *intellectual disability* is the equivalent term for the ICD-11 diagnosis of *intellectual developmental disorders*. Although the term *intellectual disability* is used throughout this manual, both terms are used in the title to clarify relationships with other classification systems. Moreover, a federal statue in the United States (Public Law 111-256, Rosa's Law) replaced the term *mental retardation* with *intellectual disability,* and research journals use the term *intellectual disability.* Thus, *intellectual disability* is the term in common use by medical, educational, and other professions and by the lay public and advocacy groups.

Specify current severity:

Mild
Moderate
Severe
Profound

Diagnostic Criteria for Autism Spectrum Disorder

A. Persistent deficits in social communication and social interaction across multiple contexts, as manifested by the following, currently or by history (examples are illustrative, not exhaustive):
   1. Deficits in social-emotional reciprocity, ranging, for example, from abnormal social approach and failure of normal back-and-forth conversation; to reduced sharing of interest, emotions, or affect; to failure to initiate or respond to social interactions.
   2. Deficits in nonverbal communicative behaviors used for social interaction, ranging, for example, from poorly integrated verbal and nonverbal communication; to abnormalities in eye contact and body language or deficits in understanding and use of gestures; to a total lack of facial expressions and nonverbal communication.
   3. Deficits in developing, maintaining, and understanding relationships, ranging, for example, from difficulties adjusting behavior to suit various social contexts; to difficulties in sharing imaginative play or in making friends; to absence of interest in peers.

Specify current severity:

Severity is based on social communication impairments and restricted, repetitive patterns of behaviors.

B. Restricted, repetitive patterns of behavior, interests, or activities, as manifested by at least two of the following, currently or by history (examples are illustrative, not exhaustive):
   1. Stereotyped or repetitive motor movements, use of objects, or speech (e.g., simple motor stereotypes, lining up toys or flipping objects, echolalia, idiosyncratic phrases).

2. Insistence on sameness, inflexible adherence to routines, or ritualized patterns of verbal or nonverbal behavior (e.g., extreme distress at small changes, difficulties with transitions, rigid thinking patterns, greeting rituals, need to take same route or eat same food every day).
3. Highly restricted, fixated interests that are abnormal in intensity or focus (e.g., strong attachment to or preoccupation with unusual objects, excessively circumscribed or perseverative interests).
4. Hyper- or hypo-reactivity to sensory input or unusual interest in sensory aspects of the environment (e.g., apparent indifference to pain/temperature, adverse response to specific sounds or textures, excessive smelling or touching of objects, visual fascination with lights or movement).

Specify current severity:

Severity is based on social communication impairments and restricted, repetitive patterns of behavior.

C. Symptoms must be present in the early developmental period (but may not become fully manifest until social demands exceed limited capacities, or may be masked by learned strategies in later life).

D. Symptoms cause clinically significant impairment in social, occupational, or other important areas of current functioning.

E. These disturbances are not better explained by intellectual disability (intellectual developmental disorder) or global developmental delay. Intellectual disability and autism spectrum disorder frequently co-occur; to make comorbid diagnoses of autism spectrum disorder and intellectual disability, social communication should be below that expected for general developmental level.

Note: Individuals with a well-established DSM-IV diagnosis of autistic disorder, Asperger's disorder, or pervasive developmental disorder not otherwise specified should be given the diagnosis of autism spectrum disorder. Individuals who have marked deficits in social communication, but whose symptoms do not otherwise meet criteria for autism spectrum disorder, should be evaluated for social (pragmatic) communication disorder.

Specify if:

With or without accompanying intellectual impairment
With or without accompanying language impairment
Associated with a known medical or genetic condition or environmental factor

Associated with another neurodevelopmental, mental, or behavioral disorder
With catatonia

Diagnostic Criteria for Attention-Deficit/Hyperactivity Disorder

A. A persistent pattern of inattention and/or hyperactivity-impulsivity that interferes with functioning or development, as characterized by (1) and/or (2):

1. **Inattention:** Six (or more) of the following symptoms have persisted for at least 6 months to a degree that is inconsistent with developmental level and that negatively impacts directly on social and academic/occupational activities:

Note: The symptoms are not solely a manifestation of oppositional behavior, defiance, hostility, or failure to understand tasks or instruction. For older adolescents and adults (age 17 and older), at least five symptoms are required.

a. Often fails to give close attention to details or makes careless mistakes in schoolwork, at work, or during other activities (e.g., overlooks or misses details, work is inaccurate).
b. Often has difficulty sustaining attention in tasks or play activities (e.g., has difficulty remaining focused during lectures, conversations, or lengthy reading).
c. Often does not seem to listen when spoken to directly (e.g., mind seems elsewhere, even in the absence of any obvious distraction).
d. Often does not follow through on instructions and fails to finish schoolwork, chores, or duties in the workplace (e.g., starts tasks but quickly loses focus and is easily sidetracked).
e. Often has difficulty organizing tasks and activities (e.g., difficulty managing sequential tasks; difficulty keeping materials and belongings in order; messy, disorganized work; has poor time management; fails to meet deadlines).
f. Often avoids, dislikes, or is reluctant to engage in tasks that require sustained mental effort (e.g., schoolwork or homework; for older adolescents and adults, preparing reports, completing forms, reviewing lengthy papers).
g. Often loses things necessary for tasks or activities (e.g., school materials, pencils, books, tools, wallets, keys, paperwork, eyeglasses, mobile telephones).

h. Is often easily distracted by extraneous stimuli (for older adolescents and adults, may include unrelated thoughts).
i. Is often forgetful in daily activities (e.g., doing chores, running errands; for older adolescents and adults, returning calls, paying bills, keeping appointments).

2. **Hyperactivity and impulsivity:** Six (or more) of the following symptoms have persisted for at least 6 months to a degree that is inconsistent with developmental level and that negatively impacts directly on social and academic/occupational activities:

Note: The symptoms are not solely a manifestation of oppositional behavior, defiance, hostility, or a failure to understand tasks or instructions. For older adolescents and adults (age 17 and older), at least five symptoms are required.

a. Often fidgets with or taps hands or feet or squirms in seat.
b. Often leaves seat in situations when remaining seated is expected (e.g., leaves his or her place in the classroom, in the office or other workplace, or in other situations that require remaining in place).
c. Often runs about or climbs in situations where it is inappropriate. (**Note:** In adolescents or adults, may be limited to feeling restless.)
d. Often unable to play or engage in leisure activities quietly.
e. Is often "on the go," acting as if "driven by a motor" (e.g., is unable to be or uncomfortable being still for extended time, as in restaurants, meetings; may be experienced by others as being restless or difficult to keep up with).
f. Often talks excessively.
g. Often blurts out an answer before a question has been completed (e.g., completes people's sentences; cannot wait for turn in conversation).
h. Often has difficulty waiting his or her turn (e.g., while waiting in line).
i. Often interrupts or intrudes on others (e.g., butts into conversations, games, or activities; may start using other people's things without asking or receiving permission; for adolescents and adults, may intrude into or take over what others are doing).

B. Several inattentive or hyperactive-impulsive symptoms were present prior to age 12 years.

C. Several inattentive or hyperactive-impulsive symptoms are present in two or more settings (e.g., at home, school, or work; with friends or relatives; in other activities).

D. There is clear evidence that the symptoms interfere with, or reduce the quality of, social, academic, or occupational functioning.

E. The symptoms do not occur exclusively during the course of schizophrenia or another psychotic disorder and are not better explained by another mental disorder (e.g., mood disorder, anxiety disorder, dissociative disorder, personality disorder, substance intoxication or withdrawal).

Specify whether:

Combined presentation: If both Criterion A1 (inattention) and Criterion A2 (hyperactivity-impulsivity) are met for the past 6 months.
Predominantly inattentive presentation: If Criterion A1 (inattention) is met but Criterion A2 (hyperactivity-impulsivity) is not met for the past 6 months.
Predominantly hyperactive/impulsive presentation: If Criterion A2 (hyperactivity-impulsivity) is met and Criterion A1 (inattention) is not met for the past 6 months.

Specify if:

In partial remission: When full criteria were previously met, fewer than the full criteria have been met for the past 6 months, and the symptoms still result in impairment in social, academic, or occupational functioning.

Specify current severity:

Mild: Few, if any, symptoms in excess of those required to make the diagnosis are present, and symptoms result in no more than minor impairments in social or occupational functioning.
Moderate: Symptoms or functional impairment between "mild" and "severe" are present.
Severe: Many symptoms in excess of those required to make the diagnosis, or several symptoms that are particularly severe, are present, or the symptoms result in marked impairment in social or occupational functioning.

Diagnostic Criteria for Conduct Disorder

A. A repetitive and persistent pattern of behavior in which the basic rights of others or major age-appropriate societal norms or rules are violated, as manifested by the presence of at least three of the following 15 criteria in the past 12 months from any of the categories below, with at least one criterion present in the past 6 months:

Aggression to People and Animals

1. Often bullies, threatens, or intimidates others.
2. Often initiates physical fights.
3. Has used a weapon that can cause serious physical harm to other (e.g., a bat, brick, broken bottle, knife, gun).
4. Has been physically cruel to people.
5. Has been physically cruel to animals.
6. Has stolen while confronting a victim (e.g., mugging, purse snatching, extortion, armed robbery).
7. Has forced someone into sexual activity.

Destruction of Property

8. Has deliberately engaged in fire setting with the intention of causing serious damage.
9. Has deliberately destroyed others' property (other than by fire setting).

Deceitfulness or Theft

10. Has broken into someone else's house, building, or car.
11. Often lies to obtain goods or favors or to avoid obligations (i.e., "cons" others).
12. Has stolen items of nontrivial value without confronting a victim (e.g., shoplifting, but without breaking and entering; forgery).

Serious Violations of Rules

13. Often stays out at night despite parental prohibitions, beginning before age 13 years.
14. Has run away from home overnight at least twice when living in the parental or parental surrogate home, or once without returning for a lengthy period.
15. Is often truant from school, beginning before age 13 years.

B. The disturbance in behavior causes clinically significant impairment in social, academic, or occupational functioning.

C. If the individual is age 18 years or older, criteria are not met for antisocial personality disorder.

Specify whether:

Childhood-onset type: Individuals show at least one symptom characteristic of conduct disorder prior to age 10 years.
Adolescent-onset type: Individuals show no symptom characteristic of conduct disorder prior to age 10 years.
Unspecified onset: Criteria for a diagnosis of conduct disorder are met, but there is not enough information available to determine whether the onset of the first symptom was before or after age 10 years.

Specify if:

With limited prosocial emotions: To qualify for this specifier, an individual must have displayed at least two of the following characteristics persistently over at least 12 months and in multiple relationships and settings. These characteristics reflect the individual's typical pattern of interpersonal and emotional functioning over this period and not just occasional occurrences in some situations. Thus, to assess the criteria for the specifier, multiple information sources are necessary. In addition to the individual's self-report, it is necessary to consider reports by others who have known the individual for extended periods of time (e.g., parents, teachers, co-workers, extended family members, peers).

> **Lack of remorse or guilt:** Does not feel bad or guilty when he or she does something wrong (exclude remorse when expressed only when caught and/or facing punishments). The individual shows a general lack of concern about the negative consequences of his or her actions. For example, the individual is not remorseful after hurting someone or does not care about the consequences of breaking rules.
> **Callous—lack of empathy:** Disregards and is unconcerned about the feelings of others. The individual is described as cold and uncaring. The person appears more concerned about the effects of his or her actions on himself or herself, rather than their effects on others, even when they result in substantial harm to others.
> **Unconcerned about performance:** Does not show concern about poor/problematic performance at school, at work, or in other important activities. The individual does not put forth the effort necessary to perform well, even when expectations are clear, and typically blames others for his or her poor performance.
> **Shallow or deficient affect:** Does not express feelings or show emotions to others, except in ways that seem shallow, insincere, or superficial (e.g., actions contradict the emotion displayed; can turn emotions "on" or "off" quickly) or when emotional expressions are used for gain (e.g., emotions displayed to manipulate or intimidate others).

Specify current severity:

Mild: Few if any conduct problems in excess of those required to make the diagnosis are present, and conduct problems cause relatively minor harm to others (e.g., lying, truancy, staying out after dark without permission, other rule breaking).
Moderate: The number of conduct problems and the effect on others are intermediate between those specified in "mild" and those in "severe" (e.g., stealing without confronting a victim, vandalism).
Severe: Many conduct problems in excess of those required to make the diagnosis are present, or conduct problems cause considerable harm to others (e.g., forced

sex, physical cruelty, use of a weapon, stealing while confronting a victim, breaking and entering).

Diagnostic Criteria for Major or Mild Neurocognitive Disorder due to Alzheimer's Disease

A. The criteria are met for major or mild neurocognitive disorder.

B. There is insidious onset and gradual progression of impairment in one or more cognitive domains (for major neurocognitive disorder, at least two domains must be impaired).

C. Criteria are met for either probable or possible Alzheimer's disease as follows:

For major neurocognitive disorder:

Probable Alzheimer's disease is diagnosed if either of the following is present; otherwise, **possible Alzheimer's disease** should be diagnosed.

1. Evidence of a causative Alzheimer's disease genetic mutation from family history or genetic testing.
2. All three of the following are present:
    a. Clear evidence of decline in memory and learning and at least one other cognitive domain (based on detailed history or serial neuropsychological testing).
    b. Steadily progressive, gradual decline in cognition, without extended plateaus.
    c. No evidence of mixed etiology (i.e., absence of other neurodegenerative or cerebrovascular disease, or another neurological, mental, or systemic disease or condition likely contributing to cognitive decline).

For mild neurocognitive disorder:

Probable Alzheimer's disease is diagnosed if there is evidence of a causative Alzheimer's disease genetic mutation from either genetic testing or family history.

Possible Alzheimer's disease is diagnosed if there is no evidence of a causative Alzheimer's disease genetic mutation from either genetic testing or family history, and all three of the following are present:

1. Clear evidence of decline in memory and learning.
2. Steadily progressive, gradual decline in cognition, without extended plateaus.
3. No evidence of mixed etiology (i.e., absence of other neurodegenerative or cerebrovascular disease, or another

neurological or systemic disease or condition likely contributing to cognitive decline).

D. The disturbance is not better explained by cerebrovascular disease, another neurodegenerative disease, the effects of a substance, or another mental, neurological, or systemic disorder.

Diagnostic Criteria for Adjustment Disorders

A. The development of emotional or behavioral symptoms in response to an identifiable stressor(s) occurring within 3 months of the onset of the stressor(s).

B. These symptoms or behaviors are clinically significant, as evidenced by one or both of the following:

  1. Marked distress that is out of proportion to the severity or intensity of the stressor, taking into account the external context and the cultural factors that might influence symptom severity and presentation.
  2. Significant impairment in social, occupational, or other important areas of functioning.

C. The stress-related disturbance does not meet the criteria for another mental disorder and is not merely an exacerbation of a preexisting mental disorder.

D. The symptoms do not represent normal bereavement.

E. Once the stressor or its consequences have terminated, the symptoms do not persist for more than an additional 6 months.

Specify whether:

With depressed mood: Low mood, tearfulness, or feelings of hopelessness are predominant.
With anxiety: Nervousness, worry, jitteriness, or separation anxiety is predominant.
With mixed anxiety and depressed mood: A combination of depression and anxiety is predominant.
With disturbance of conduct: Disturbance of conduct is predominant.
With mixed disturbance of emotions and conduct: Both emotional symptoms (e.g., depression, anxiety) and a disturbance of conduct are predominant.
Unspecified: For maladaptive reactions that are not classifiable as one of the specific subtypes of adjustment disorder.

Diagnostic Criteria for Gambling Disorder

A. Persistent and recurrent problematic gambling behavior leading to clinically significant impairment or distress, as indicated by the individual exhibiting four (or more) of the following in a 12-month period:

1. Needs to gamble with increasing amounts of money in order to achieve the desired excitement.
2. Is restless or irritable when attempting to cut down or stop gambling.
3. Has made repeated unsuccessful efforts to control, cut back, or stop gambling.
4. Is often preoccupied with gambling (e.g., having persistent thoughts of reliving past gambling experiences, handicapping or planning the next venture, thinking of ways to get money with which to gamble).
5. Often gambles when feeling distressed (e.g., helpless, guilty, anxious, depressed).
6. After losing money gambling, often returns another day to get even ("chasing" one's losses).
7. Lies to conceal the extent of involvement with gambling.
8. Has jeopardized or lost a significant relationship, job, or educational or career opportunity because of gambling.
9. Relies on others to provide money to relieve desperate financial situations caused by gambling.

B. The gambling behavior is not better explained by a manic episode.

Specify if:

Episodic: Meeting diagnostic criteria at more than one time point, with symptoms subsiding between periods of gambling disorder for at least several months.
Persistent: Experiencing continuous symptoms, to meet diagnostic criteria for multiple years.

Specify if:

In early remission: After full criteria for gambling disorder were previously met, none of the criteria for gambling disorder have been met for at least 3 months but for less than 12 months.
In sustained remission: After full criteria for gambling disorder were previously met, none of the criteria for gambling disorder have been met during a period of 12 months or longer.

Specify current severity:

Mild: 4-5 criteria met.
Moderate: 6-7 criteria met.
Severe: 8-9 criteria met.

Diagnostic Criteria for Premenstrual Dysphoric Disorder

A. In the majority of menstrual cycles, at least five symptoms must be present in the final week before the onset of menses, start to *improve* within a few days after the onset of menses, and become *minimal* or absent in the week postmenses.

B. One (or more) of the following symptoms must be present:
   1. Marked affective lability (e.g., mood swings; feeling suddenly sad or tearful, or increased sensitivity to rejection).
   2. Marked irritability or anger or increased interpersonal conflicts.
   3. Marked depressed mood, feelings of hopelessness, or self-deprecating thoughts.
   4. Marked anxiety, tension, and/or feelings of being keyed up or on edge.

C. One (or more) of the following symptoms must additionally be present, to reach a total of *five* symptoms when combined with symptoms from Criterion B above.
   1. Decreased interest in usual activities (e.g., work, school, friends, hobbies).
   2. Subjective difficulty in concentration.
   3. Lethargy, easy fatigability, or marked lack of energy.
   4. Marked change in appetite; overeating; or specific food cravings.
   5. Hypersomnia or insomnia.
   6. A sense of being overwhelmed or out of control.
   7. Physical symptoms such as breast tenderness or swelling, joint or muscle pain, a sensation of "bloating," or weight gain.

Note: The symptoms in Criteria A-C must have been met for most menstrual cycles that occurred in the preceding year.

D. The symptoms are associated with clinically significant distress or interference with work, school, usual social activities, or relationships with others (e.g., avoidance of social activities; decreased productivity and efficiency at work, school, or home).

E. The disturbance is not merely an exacerbation of the symptoms of another disorder, such as major depressive disorder, panic disorder, persistent depressive disorder (dysthymia), or a personality disorder (although it may co-occur with any of these disorders).

F. Criterion A should be confirmed by prospective daily ratings during at least two symptomatic cycles. (**Note:** The diagnosis may be made provisionally prior to this confirmation.)

G. The symptoms are not attributable to the physiological effects of a substance (e.g., a drug of abuse, a medication, other treatment) or another medical condition (e.g., hyperthyroidism).

Diagnostic Criteria for Factitious Disorder Imposed on Another (Previously Factitious Disorder by Proxy)

A. Falsification of physical or psychological signs or symptoms, or induction of injury or disease, in another, associated with identified deception.

B. The individual presents another individual (victim) to others as ill, impaired, or injured.

C. The deceptive behavior is evident even in the absence of obvious external rewards.

D. The behavior is not better explained by another mental disorder, such as delusional disorder or another psychotic disorder.

Note: The perpetrator, not the victim, receives this diagnosis.

Specify:

Single episode
Recurrent episodes (two or more events of falsification of illness and/or induction of injury)

DIAGNOSTIC CRITERIA FOR PERSONALITY DISORDERS

CLUSTER A PERSONALITY DISORDERS

Paranoid Personality Disorder

A. A pervasive distrust and suspiciousness of others such that their motives are interpreted as malevolent, beginning by early adulthood and present in a variety of contexts, as indicated by four (or more) of the following:
   1. Suspects, without sufficient basis, that others are exploiting, harming, or deceiving him or her.
   2. Is preoccupied with unjustified doubts about the loyalty or trustworthiness of friends or associates.
   3. Is reluctant to confide in others because of unwarranted fear that the information will be used maliciously against him or her.
   4. Reads hidden demeaning or threatening meanings into benign remarks or events.
   5. Persistently bears grudges (i.e., is unforgiving of insults, injuries, or slights).
   6. Perceives attacks on his or her character or reputation that are not apparent to others and is quick to react angrily or to counterattack.
   7. Has recurrent suspicions, without justification, regarding fidelity of spouse or sexual partner.

B. Does not occur exclusively during the course of schizophrenia, a bipolar disorder or depressive disorder with psychotic features, or another psychotic disorder and is not attributable to the physiological effects of another medical condition.

Note: If criteria are met prior to the onset of schizophrenia, add "premorbid," i.e., "paranoid personality disorder (premorbid)."

Schizoid Personality Disorder

A. A pervasive pattern of detachment from social relationships and a restricted range of expression of emotions in interpersonal settings, beginning by early adulthood and present in a variety of contexts, as indicated by four (or more) of the following:

1. Neither desires nor enjoys close relationships, including being part of a family.
2. Almost always chooses solitary activities.
3. Has little, if any, interest in having sexual experiences with another person.
4. Takes pleasure in few, if any, activities.
5. Lacks close friends or confidants other than first-degree relatives.
6. Appears indifferent to the praise or criticism of others.
7. Shows emotional coldness, detachment, or flattened affectivity.

B. Does not occur exclusively during the course of schizophrenia, a bipolar disorder of depressive disorder with psychotic feature, another psychotic disorder, or autism spectrum disorder and is not attributable to the physiological effects of another medical condition.

Note: If criteria are met prior to the onset of schizophrenia, add "premorbid," i.e. "schizoid personality disorder (premorbid)."

Schizotypal Personality Disorder

A. A pervasive pattern of social and interpersonal deficits marked by acute discomfort with, and reduced capacity for, close relationships as well as by cognitive or perceptual distortions and eccentricities of behavior, beginning by early adulthood and present in a variety of contexts, as indicated by five (or more) of the following:

1. Ideas of reference (excluding delusions of reference).
2. Odd beliefs or magical thinking that influences behavior and is inconsistent with subcultural norms (e.g., superstitiousness, belief in clairvoyance, telepathy, or "sixth sense"; in children and adolescents, bizarre fantasies or preoccupations).
3. Unusual perceptual experiences, including bodily illusions.
4. Odd thinking and speech (e.g., vague, circumstantial, metaphorical overelaborate, or stereotyped).
5. Suspiciousness or paranoid ideation.
6. Inappropriate or constricted affect.
7. Behavior or appearance that is odd, eccentric, or peculiar.
8. Lack of close friends or confidants other than first-degree relatives
9. Excessive social anxiety that does not diminish with familiarity and tends to be associated with paranoid fears rather than negative judgments about self.

B. Does not occur exclusively during the course of schizophrenia, a bipolar disorder or depressive disorder with psychotic features, another psychotic disorder, or autism spectrum disorder.

Note: If criteria are met prior to the onset of schizophrenia, add "premorbid," e.g., "schizotypal personality disorder (premorbid)."

CLUSTER B PERSONALITY DISORDERS

Antisocial Personality Disorder

A. A pervasive pattern of disregard for and violation of the rights of others, occurring since age 15 years, as indicated by three (or more) of the following:
   1. Failure to conform to social norms with respect to lawful behaviors, as indicated by repeatedly performing acts that are grounds for arrest.
   2. Deceitfulness, as indicated by repeated lying, use of aliases, or conning others for personal profit or pleasure.
   3. Impulsivity or failure to plan ahead.
   4. Irritability and aggressiveness, as indicated by repeated physical fights or assaults.
   5. Reckless disregard for safety of self or others.
   6. Consistent irresponsibility, as indicated by repeated failure to sustain consistent work behavior or honor financial obligations.
   7. Lack of remorse, as indicated by being indifferent to or rationalizing having hurt, mistreated, or stolen from another.

B. The individual is at least age 18 years.

C. There is evidence of conduct disorder with onset before age 15 years.

D. The occurrence of antisocial behavior is not exclusively during the course of schizophrenia or bipolar disorder.

Borderline Personality Disorder

A pervasive pattern of instability of interpersonal relationships, self-image, and affects, and marked impulsivity, beginning by early adulthood and present in a variety of contexts, as indicated by five (or more) of the following:

1. Frantic efforts to avoid real or imagined abandonment. (**Note:** Do not include suicidal or self-mutilating behavior covered in Criterion 5.)
2. A pattern of unstable and intense interpersonal relationships characterized by alternating between extremes of idealization and devaluation.
3. Identity disturbance: markedly and persistently unstable self-image or sense of self.
4. Impulsivity in at least two areas that are potentially self-damaging (e.g., spending, sex, substance abuse, reckless driving, binge eating). (**Note:** Do not include suicidal or self-mutilating behavior covered in Criterion 5.)
5. Recurrent suicidal behavior, gestures, or threats, or self-mutilating behavior.
6. Affective instability due to a marked reactivity of mood (e.g., intense episodic dysphoria, irritability, or anxiety usually lasting a few hours and only rarely more than a few days).
7. Chronic feelings of emptiness.
8. Inappropriate, intense anger or difficulty controlling anger (e.g., frequent displays of temper, constant anger, recurrent physical fights).
9. Transient, stress-related paranoid ideation or severe dissociative symptoms.

Histrionic Personality Disorder

A pervasive pattern of excessive emotionally and attention seeking, beginning by early adulthood and present in a variety of contexts, as indicated by five (or more) of the following:

1. Is uncomfortable in situations in which he or she is not the center of attention.
2. Interaction with others is often characterized by inappropriate sexually seductive or provocative behavior.
3. Displays rapidly shifting and shallow expression of emotions.
4. Consistently uses physical appearance to draw attention to self.
5. Has a style of speech that is excessively impressionistic and lacking in detail.
6. Shows self-dramatization, theatricality, and exaggerated expression of emotion.
7. Is suggestible (i.e., easily influenced by others or circumstances).
8. Considers relationships to be more intimate than they actually are.

Narcissistic Personality Disorder

A pervasive pattern of grandiosity (in fantasy or behavior), need for admiration, and lack of empathy, beginning by early adulthood and present in a variety of contexts, as indicated by five (or more) of the following:

1. Has a grandiose sense of self-importance (e.g., exaggerates achievements and talents, expects to be recognized as superior without commensurate achievements).
2. Is preoccupied with fantasies of unlimited success, power, brilliance, beauty, or ideal love.
3. Believes that he or she is "special" and unique and can only be understood by, or should associate with, other special or high-status people (or institutions).
4. Requires excessive admiration.
5. Has a sense of entitlement (i.e., unreasonable expectations of especially favorable treatment or automatic compliance with his or her expectations).
6. Is interpersonally exploitative (i.e., takes advantage of others to achieve his or her own ends).
7. Lacks empathy: is unwilling to recognize or identify with the feelings and needs of others.
8. Is often envious of others or believes that others are envious of him or her.
9. Shows arrogant, haughty behaviors or attitudes.

CLUSTER C PERSONALITY DISORDERS

Avoidant Personality Disorder

A pervasive pattern of social inhibition, feelings of inadequacy, and hypersensitivity to negative evaluation, beginning by early adulthood and present in a variety of contexts, as indicated by four (or more) of the following:

1. Avoids occupational activities that involve significant interpersonal contact because of fears of criticism, disapproval, or rejection.
2. Is unwilling to get involved with people unless certain of being liked.

3. Shows restraint within intimate relationships because of the fear of being shamed or ridiculed.
4. Is preoccupied with being criticized or rejected in social situations.
5. Is inhibited in new interpersonal situations because of feelings of inadequacy.
6. Views self as socially inept, personally unappealing, or inferior to others.
7. Is unusually reluctant to take personal risks or to engage in any new activities because they may prove embarrassing.

Dependent Personality Disorder

A pervasive and excessive need to be taken care of that leads to submissive and clinging behavior and fears of separation, beginning by early adulthood and present in a variety of contexts, as indicated by five (or more) of the following:

1. Has difficulty making everyday decisions without an excessive amount of advice and reassurance from others.
2. Needs others to assume responsibility for most major areas of his or her life.
3. Has difficulty expressing disagreement with others because of fear of loss of support or approval. (**Note**: Do not include realistic fears of retribution.)
4. Has difficulty initiating projects or doing things on his or her own (because of a lack of self-confidence in judgment or abilities rather than a lack of motivation or energy).
5. Goes to excessive lengths to obtain nurturance and support from others, to the point of volunteering to do things that are unpleasant.
6. Feels uncomfortable or helpless when alone because of exaggerated fears of being unable to care for himself or herself.
7. Urgently seeks another relationship as a source of care and support when a close relationship ends.
8. Is unrealistically preoccupied with fears of being left to take care of himself or herself.

Obsessive-Compulsive Personality Disorder

A pervasive pattern of preoccupation with orderliness, perfectionism, and mental and interpersonal control, at the expense of flexibility, openness, and efficiency, beginning by early adulthood and present in a variety of contexts, as indicated by four (or more) of the following:

1. Is preoccupied with details, rules, lists, order, organization, or schedules to the extent that the major point of the activity is lost.
2. Shows perfectionism that interferes with task completion (e.g., is unable to complete a project because his or her own overly strict standards are not met).
3. Is excessively devoted to work and productivity to the exclusion of leisure activities and friendships (not accounted for by obvious economic necessity).
4. Is overconscientious, scrupulous, and inflexible about matters of morality, ethics, or values (not accounted for by cultural or religious identification).
5. Is unable to discard worn-out or worthless objects even when they have no sentimental value.
6. Is reluctant to delegate tasks or to work with others unless they submit to exactly his or her way of doing things.
7. Adopts a miserly spending style toward both self and others; money is viewed as something to be hoarded for future catastrophes.
8. Shows rigidity and stubbornness.

CASE EXAMPLES

The following clinical cases are presented in the format of a psychological assessment report and include DSM diagnoses. This material is authentic in that it is based on information provided by individuals seeking psychological services in Canadian mental health treatment facilities. Identifying characteristics have been removed or disguised out of respect for the privacy of those described, and some creative license has been taken to ensure the flow of the narrative. Characteristics of two or more clients may have been combined to further distort identifying information; however, efforts have been taken to retain the clinical flavour and general context of the cases.

Case #1

Brian was a 24-year-old man who was referred for a neuropsychological outpatient assessment by his treating psychiatrist who was concerned about the extent of Brian's odd thinking and behavior, and was seeking recommendations for rehabilitation planning. Even though Brian was a relatively young man, he had already spent the past several years with little productivity: not attending school, not working, and living in shelters or in a boarding home. There had been a previous psychiatric hospitalization of two to three months' duration related to bizarre thinking and unusual behaviour.

He was born in rural Ontario, the second eldest of four boys in a highly educated family; his father was a physician and his mother had a doctorate in philosophy. There were frequent moves when he was a youngster related to his parent's educational training and initial jobs but eventually the family settled in a city in southwestern Ontario. Brian was always a shy loner; he kept to himself and would spend hours daydreaming or sometimes drawing, mainly sketches of objects. As he grew older, he discovered the guitar and would strum for hours at a time, mostly "random" chords rather than specific songs. His school performance was considered average; he rarely spoke in class. When teachers did call upon him, they were at times amazed by his articulate vocabulary, while at other times they found his answers to be vague and off-topic. He was not disruptive in the classroom, rather his gaze seemed to wander; he enjoyed the window seat where he preferred to look at the sky rather than at the teacher or classmates. In fact, he had no friends at all. There was a single sexual encounter with a girl who felt "sorry" for him and kissed him; he remained detached and unresponsive. Over time, during his final high school year, Brian became increasingly withdrawn and "unreachable"; he was indifferent to attempts to engage him in conversation. Not overtly tearful or sad, his face seemed impenetrable with remarkably little demonstrated affect. He often looked in a daze and had a blank expression. His school work deteriorated; he was skipping classes and at one point, the principal discovered him wandering aimlessly in the parking lot. He was admitted to hospital in part out of concern for his ability to care for himself and also to investigate his mental and emotional state. Interviewing him was extremely challenging; he was slow to respond and had trouble focusing. There was evidence of "thought blocking"; he later admitted that he felt as though someone had stolen the idea from his head. He eventually acknowledged beliefs that he had special powers "to do almost anything satanically". He found he would avoid watching television news programs because of the messages that seemed addressed to him, that the police were about to conduct an investigation regarding a pear that he had taken years ago that had dropped from a neighbour's tree. Admission blood and urine tests failed to identify any alcohol or substance use; he denied ever trying street drugs. He was treated with anti-psychotic medication and asked to participate in group sessions on the ward. He sat in virtual silence, literally keeping his distance by sitting in the chair farthest from others. He seemed wary and defensive, deflecting inquiries by stating that it was the other people in the group who seemed "paranoid".

He was discharged after a few months to live in a supervised boarding home. He found that he disliked sharing a room with someone else and having to eat meals with others. He felt nauseous one morning and developed an idea that his food had been poisoned. He remained there for several more months and then left against advice to live in a downtown homeless shelter, supported by monthly government social assistance.

With the supportive reminders from his parents, he maintained weekly contact with a community health clinic case worker and monthly meetings with an outpatient psychiatrist who spent over a year attempting to "engage" him in a therapeutic process. They suggested that he undergo a neuropsychological assessment and he eventually agreed.

Brian had to be encouraged to attend the assessment since from his own perspective, he did not feel that there were any serious problems. He missed the first appointment and then attended the second interview only after a reminder call was made that morning to the place where he was living. He appeared disheveled and lacked good hygiene; he wore a stained t-shirt and his hair was uncombed. Rapport was difficult to establish; in fact, he later acknowledged that "I thought that I was going to be interacting with machines". Most striking was his variable attention. At times he seemed hyper-vigilant, that is, staring intently and highly focused with acute notice of intricate detail, while at other times he seemed perplexed and distracted, stating "I'm drifting". Neuropsychological test results discovered remarkable deficits on tests that measure attention and concentration; he could manage only very limited verbal learning. There were strengths evident on drawing tasks as well as superb rhythm perception. Projective personality tests showed bizarre verbalization responses of incongruous combinations ("mutant butterfly with the characteristics of an ant") and an absence of any human images.

Brian's DSM-5 diagnoses are as follows:

Schizophrenia

Schizoid Personality Disorder (Premorbid)

Psychosis Symptom Severity

Psychosis Domain: Delusions were rated initially as present and severe (4)

He met the DSM-5 (American Psychiatric Association, 2013) diagnostic criteria for Schizophrenia. He had both delusions and hallucinations (Criterion A), with paranoid ideas that were evident for more than a month, though these became less prominent with medication treatment. There was social/occupational dysfunction (Criterion B), and continuous signs of disturbance over at least a six-month period (Criterion C). He was not showing mood disorder (Exclusion Criterion D) and did not use alcohol or street drugs (Exclusion Criterion E). There was no pervasive development disorder (Exclusion Criterion F).

He was diagnosed with Schizoid Personality Disorder with the added designation of "premorbid" indicated in this case because the criteria were met prior to the onset of schizophrenia symptoms. He showed at least four of the seven criteria, including his avoidance of close relations, his tendency to choose solitary activities, his lack of close friends and the sense of interpersonal detachment. Some theoretical perspectives suggest that a schizoid personality pattern (and perhaps other related patterns described colloquially as "shyness") may be phenotypic foreshadows for the onset of schizophrenia in adulthood.

Based on the DSM-5 Section III, there was an opportunity to evaluate his progress using the Clinician-Rated Dimensions of Psychosis Symptom Severity. Ratings of his delusions highlighted the change from an initial score of 4 (present and severe) to a score of 2 (present but mild).

A criticism made over the years by some psychologists of the DSM criteria is that there remains a failure in the psychiatric nomenclature to integrate decades of neuropsychological research findings which have identified cognitive deficits associated with schizophrenia. The DSM-5 Section III does allow now an opportunity to rate his general level of cognition, which in this circumstance, would be considered mildly to moderately impaired, however, such global ratings add only marginally to painting the complete clinical picture. In this case example, the neuropsychological assessment contributed to understanding Brian's condition through identifying so-called "hidden" strengths in the non-verbal area which were not entirely obvious to others; strengths in visual planning which allow to him to shine in his artistic pursuits; and strengths in his rhythm perception which contribute to his musical talents. Further, the neuropsychological assessment identified areas of impairment in the areas of concentration and working memory which contribute to being inattentive and easily distracted. The clarification of these cognitive deficits helped his family and his rehabilitation therapist to become more understanding when he seemed to them to be "resistant" on occasions when there were complicated demands; they came to understand that he was not being defiant but rather he was clearly struggling to absorb the information.

He began attending rehabilitation programs including weekly classes in social skills training and twice-weekly sessions at a local "consumer/client-run" art studio dedicated to people with serious mental illness. He sold his first piece of art at an exhibition sponsored by a local "mental health consumer" group and gave a guitar performance at a talent show organized by his rehabilitation program. With the support of his rehabilitation case manager, he found an apartment with subsidized rent that he could afford and is now living on his own, attending a weekly collective kitchen program in which he receives support to make his dinner meals.

Case #2

Branka is a 32-year-old woman who was referred for a psychological outpatient assessment by her treating physician due to her slow recovery from pain symptoms that began after she was injured in a motor vehicle accident. Her physician had diagnosed whiplash strain injuries that were causing pain discomfort in her neck and lower back and referred her for physiotherapy treatment. She was refusing to attend however, because she was too frightened to drive and was avoiding any vehicle travel unless absolutely necessary. As a passenger she would become a "back-seat driver", screaming to be careful, constantly mirror-checking and clenching her fists. It was now over a month since the accident and she was still having trouble sleeping, and admitted tearfully that she wanted to stay home but also did not want to be left alone due to a sense of foreboding. Her physician was seeking advice about the nature of her psychological difficulties and recommendations for treatment.

She was flustered when she arrived for the interview, seeming tense and mildly agitated. It took some time before she settled; in particular, she was quite reluctant to talk about the accident itself. She described feeling "useless" around the house, how she felt uncharacteristically uninvolved in family meal conversation, like she had a numbing of feelings. She admitted a sense of apprehension that something bad might happen to her whole family and that she would be unable to help. She worried about returning to her job as a personal caregiver, fearing that she might not be able to handle a crisis. On the other hand, she fretted that without the income from her job, her family would suffer financially; she seemed almost paralyzed with ambivalence over returning to work, not sure what to do. Further, she was self-protective about her bodily movements, fearing re-injury, despite reassurance from her physician that increased activity would actually enhance her recovery. With encouragement, she was able to disclose her recollections of the accident. She described how she was driving home from work at dusk and was stopped in a line of traffic at a light which had changed but the traffic had not moved. As she glanced in her rear-view mirror, she saw that a large truck was barreling towards her. She tightened her grip on the steering wheel and tensed herself, thinking "I am going to die". Most vivid to her was the staring headlights of the truck and sound of the crash, which to her seemed like an explosion. She was taken by ambulance to hospital where she was examined, x-rays were taken (there were no fractures) and she was released for follow-up the next day with her family doctor. Upon further inquiry, she was questioned about whether there were any other details about the accident which she had missed. She pondered this for some time and began sobbing. She reported that the reason the traffic had not moved was that she saw there was a pedestrian still crossing the street; she feared for the person's life as well as for her own, feeling helpless with the impending crash.

In terms of her personal history, she was born in what was to become a civil-war torn country in Eastern Europe, the sixth of ten children; she has nine brothers. Her father was a successful businessman; the family lived in large house on the outskirts of the city. She attended a private school, excelling in her high school studies, particularly biology and other sciences and then completing what was essentially four-year college level training in nursing. She was extremely close to her mother, who was also her best friend. In fact, she never made a decision without first asking her mother's advice. As well, despite her academic success, she avoided taking on positions of responsibility, tending to be a "follower" rather than a leader. Her mother was a dedicated homemaker devoted in every way to her children's welfare. Branka learned cooking skills from her, savouring the smells that wafted through the home upon return from school, helping her in the kitchen and talking with her about what she had learned and her eagerness about the clinical nursing placements that she had begun. The clouds of civil war however soon overshadowed what had been a seemingly idyllic life. Gun-toting rebels now roamed the streets, with tensions escalating in the country just as she had finished her placements and obtained her nursing certificate. Tragedy struck when a lone rebel gunman, someone known to the family, shot and killed her father and three older brothers. The remnants of the family retreated to their home in the countryside, avoiding trips to the city but such relatively calm refuge was short-lived. Two months after the murder of her father and brothers, a rocket launcher bomb struck their home in the middle of night, with a fiery explosion that caused walls to crash. It was a night etched in her memory, since the family had fortunately been sleeping outdoors in the courtyard due to the heat, a life-saving circumstance since the bomb destroyed the side of the home with their usual sleeping quarters. They left their home in a rush, with minimal packing; in fact, she describes a fleeting memory that her mother did not even have shoes on her feet. She recalls too her mother urging her to remain strong and to keep track of her brothers. They managed to escape to a bordering country where they remained in a refugee camp for several years ("it was still not so safe, we lived in continual fear") and then emigrated as refugees to a city in Ontario with her mother and younger brothers. With her mother's encouragement, she attended adult learning classes in English as Second Language (ESL) and also completed a personal support worker (PSW) program, with placements in senior's home.

Formal psychometric testing was only of limited value because of language and cultural issues; a culture-fair non-verbal estimate of her cognitive functions showed that she has at least Average intellect. A clinical interview review of her symptoms revealed that following the accident, she was avoiding any kinds of driving and was only traveling in a car or a taxi when necessary such as to attend medical appointments. Most terrifying to her were the nightmares that woke her up at night; she began sobbing and did not want to disclose the content of these dreams but admitted that she had images of the "worst happening". She finds herself easily startled by noises, especially the sounds of squealing brakes and truck "backfire", which she can hear from the subsidized townhouse where she lives with her mother and younger siblings. She would become quite moody around them, at times, detached while other times clinging especially with her mother and not wanting to be left alone.

Branka's DSM-5 diagnoses are as follows:

Posttraumatic Stress Disorder

Dependent Personality Disorder

She met the DSM-5 (American Psychiatric Association, 2013) diagnostic criteria for Posttraumatic Stress Disorder. She directly experienced an event in which she felt helpless and feared serious injury (Criterion A). There was event re-experiencing including nightmares and flashbacks (Criterion B), phobic avoidance and numbed responsiveness (Criteria C), blocking in recall about aspects of the event, moodiness, diminished interests and detachment (Criterion D), as well as startle responses, troubles falling asleep and hypervigilance (Criterion E), lasting over a month (Criterion F) and causing significant distress and functional impairments (Criterion G). Her condition was not attributable to the physiological effects of substance use or some other medical factor (Exclusion Criteria H).

She was diagnosed with Dependent Personality Disorder because of long-standing fears of separation that pre-dated the accident, including feeling uncomfortable being alone, lack of self-assertion and self-initiative, as well as indecisiveness and reliance on others for advice and support.

In terms of her medical condition, her treating physician diagnosed whiplash neck and back strain injuries.

Diagnosis of post-traumatic stress conditions is complicated since isolated criteria seem to appear in other conditions. The criterion of hypervigilance can be confused with the paranoid conditions, and the intrusive ideation criterion (such as flashback images) can be confused with psychotic hallucinations. Impairments in affective regulation can be confused with the kind of volatile moodiness associated with borderline personality conditions. The DSM-5 now distinguishes post-traumatic stress as a category distinct from anxiety disorders, which recognizes that trauma conditions involve negative alterations in cognitions and mood that are distinct from basic phobias or panic states.

She was referred for individual psychotherapy with a counsellor who was experienced in trauma therapy. She disclosed fears that arose not just from the car accident but fears that she had kept to herself for years since escaping her war-torn native land, associating the sound of the bright headlights and the crash with the fiery bomb experience that she had survived as a young adult. The treatment involved weekly sessions over the course of a year and included "exposure" sessions with an in-car driving therapist in which she was encouraged to return to driving. The treatment was successful in that the frequency of nightmares diminished significantly, she began sleeping better, felt more rested and was able to return to work; she remained somewhat nervous while driving, especially at intersections when she saw pedestrians crossing and when she saw a truck in her rear-view mirror.

REFERENCES

American Psychiatric Association. (2013). *Diagnostic and Statistical Manual of Mental Disorders* (5th ed.). Arlington, VA: American Psychiatric Publishing.

Davison, G.C., Flett, G.L., Blankstein, K.R., & Neale, J.M. (2014). *Abnormal Psychology: Canadian Edition* (5th ed.). Toronto: John Wiley & Sons Canada, Ltd.